Timber Decay in Buildings and its Treatment

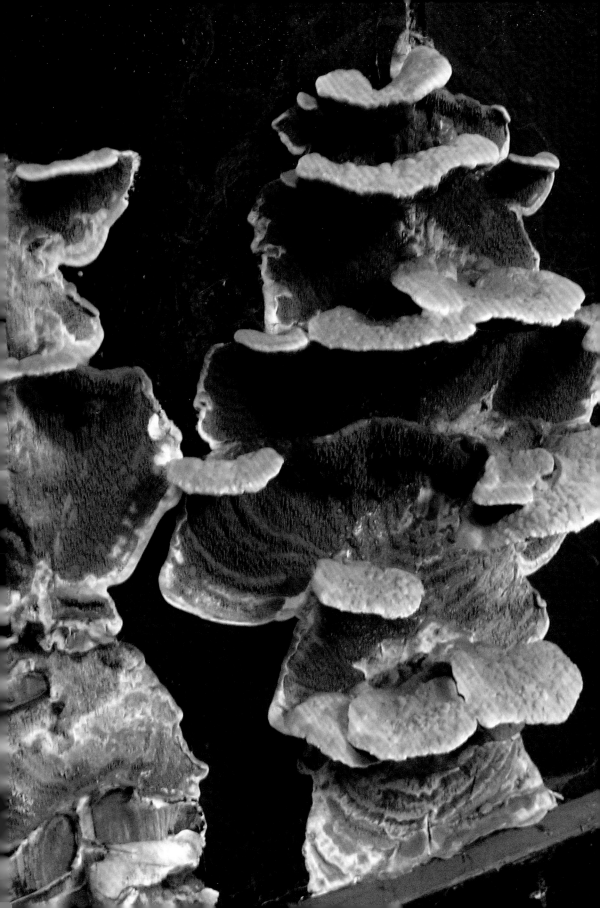

Timber Decay in Buildings and its Treatment

Brian Ridout

Historic England

Published by Historic England, The Engine House, Fire Fly Avenue, Swindon SN2 2EH
www.HistoricEngland.org.uk

Historic England is a Government service championing England's heritage and giving
expert, constructive advice.

First published 2019

ISBN 978-1-84802-539-4

British Library Cataloguing in Publication data
A CIP catalogue record for this book is available from the British Library.

Brought to publication by Sarah Enticknap, Publishing, Historic England.

Typeset in Georgia Pro 9/11pt

Edited by Kathryn Glendenning
Indexed by Caroline Jones, Osprey Indexing
Page layout by Matthew Wilson

Printed in the UK by Gomer Press

Front cover: The large circular holes from which woodwasps emerge, as well as the holes made by
furniture beetles, which provide a useful size comparison.

Frontispiece: Bracket-shaped dry rot fruits.

Contents

Foreword

Brian Ridout is an international authority on timber decay, specialising in its prevention and treatment in historic buildings. He has a long association with Historic England (previously English Heritage) and worked as a Senior Architectural Conservator in the Building Conservation & Research Team. He led its ground-breaking European research project to understand the life cycle of the deathwatch beetle and how best to deal with infestations.

Brian was the author of English Heritage's seminal book, *Timber Decay in Buildings – The conservation approach to treatment* (2000) and joint editor of the *Timber* volume in its *Practical Building Conservation series* (2012). He continues to act as a consultant to Historic England where his knowledge and experience are highly valued.

Ridout Associates, Brian's company, has provided expert advice around the world for three decades and he continues to carry out scientific assessments of timber decay and damp-related problems in historic buildings.

Timber Decay in Buildings and its Treatment provides a concise summary of the causes, treatment and prevention of timber decay in historic buildings. Its purpose is to provide readers with a clear understanding of how and why insects and fungi thrive in damp conditions and how treatments can be targeted so as to maximise their effectiveness and minimise the loss of historic fabric. Its intention is to show that chemicals and pesticides are not the answer, although it explains their use and references to the history of treatments highlight why these have proved to be so popular.

The more benign approach advocated by this book calls for a little time and thought to be spent considering the problem. Experience has shown that a great deal of apparent decay and infestation is historic and may well have ceased decades ago, when the initial problem, such as a leaking gutter, was rectified. A limited number of deathwatch beetle carcasses does not mean that a building should be opened up for invasive chemical treatments. A targeted, gradual approach is likely to be far more beneficial and far less destructive.

The use of chemical treatments and pesticides is likely to cause more damage, especially if a guarantee is required. Although these treatments can be applied quickly and in a safe manner, a genuinely 'safe' chemical treatment has yet to be found. Many of those used over the last few decades have now been found to be harmful to health and have been banned.

This book covers full treatment, limited treatment and no treatment options, and reviews the history of timber preservation to show how attitudes to treatment have evolved.

Chris Wood
Senior Architectural Conservator, Historic England

Introduction

Most wood decays eventually if it remains damp and the rapidity of its decay depends upon its durability. Durability may be inherent or artificially provided by impregnation with chemicals.

These statements take the theory of timber conservation about as far as many homeowners or professionals (builders, architects and surveyors) wish to take it. A good spray with something that says 'preservative' on the label is deemed to be a wise precaution and is thought to be particularly useful if accompanied by some sort of guarantee. The meaning of the guarantee is probably a little hazy. It might mean that timber that hasn't been infested with woodworm in 200 years will not become infested with woodworm in the next few decades; or it might mean that the treated wood will not be decayed by fungi if kept dry, something that would have been the case even without the treatment.

The result of this cheerful acceptance of perceived wisdom and trade hype has been that vast amounts of biocides have been flung unnecessarily into buildings, and teams of 'specialists' have frequently caused more damage to interiors in the pursuit of deathwatch beetle or dry rot than the organisms they sought to destroy.

Slowly, very slowly, at the close of the 20th century and the beginning of the 21st, people have begun to realise that biocides are not a panacea for all decay or infestation problems. If insects or fungi are destroying the timber within our building then biocides may be appropriate. However, we must be cautious about relying on the advice given by companies that make a living by selling remedial treatments, because this is hardly likely to be impartial.

It must be admitted that the standard approach to treatments is not entirely the industry's fault. The books on the subject that were available during the 20th century tended to be written by members of the treatment industry, with treatments in mind, and the more cautious approach to be found in the excellent Building Research Establishment publications was generally ignored.

Laboratory-based science has frequently not helped either. For example, the abilities and requirements of potentially destructive dry rot have been extensively investigated, but mostly in isolation. When dry rot is compared with the common wet rot, called cellar rot, we find that the cellar rot can tolerate drier conditions and even the much-emphasised ability of dry rot to travel through walls is shared by several other strand-producing fungi. Yes, dry rot weeps moisture if there is excess water around (*see* Fig 38) but so do some wet rots (*see* Fig 51). The conclusion is that dry rot's ability to cause considerable damage is more due to vigorous growth, under ideal conditions, than to any unusual attribute. However, the fungus does not always grow vigorously, it cannot tolerate drying and not all timbers are equally susceptible.

I remember being summoned to a house in Kent some years ago. Dry rot had grown from decayed floorboards onto the foot of a very valuable yew-wood sideboard and the remedial company was insisting that it should be burnt. In fact, all that was needed was to scrape off the fungus and move the sideboard to a dryer position where the floor was not going to collapse beneath it.

If we are to minimise damage, maximise the retention of significant fabric in our buildings and make best use of available finances then biocides must be just one of a number of tools in our workbox. They must not be allowed to replace thought and knowledge. The amount of knowledge required to make an informed judgement is actually not that great. But it does require us to abandon the notions that wood is a uniform material, that decay is inevitable if wood moisture contents rise and that organisms such as dry rot are practically indestructible and have somehow adapted to a life in buildings.

1 | Understanding the problem

1.1 Why is the durability of wood variable?

1.1.1 Softwoods and hardwoods

Commercial timbers are grouped either as softwoods or hardwoods. The term softwood is used for timber from cone-bearing, needle-leafed trees such as pines (Fig 1), while hardwood is from broad-leafed flowering trees such as oak and ash (Fig 2). The terms seem originally to have been used to differentiate between traditional hard, durable building timbers and the imported soft and more easily worked woods more suitable for interior use. This distinction is now potentially misleading, since, for example, balsa wood would be classed as a hardwood despite the fact that it is very soft, while yew is a softwood despite being rather hard. Hardwoods cannot automatically be assumed to be more durable than softwoods.

Fig 1
Scots pine, a softwood tree.

Fig 2

Oak, a hardwood tree.

1.1.2 Tree growth and natural durability

As a tree grows taller, the cambium (a layer of cells just under the bark) produces wood cells, thereby thickening the trunk (Fig 3). This new wood conducts water and nutrients and is therefore known as sapwood. The proportion of sapwood that a tree stem will ultimately contain depends on the tree species and the spread of the leafy canopy. More leaves require more water to sustain them and if this water is not available (that is, if there is not enough sapwood) the leaves will desiccate. Too much sapwood, however, would mean the tree was conducting more water than it required, which would be inefficient. This relationship between canopy spread and sapwood means that trees growing within woodland, where canopy spread is restricted, are likely to have less sapwood than trees of the same species growing at the edge of the wood.

The tree is able to maintain optimum water transportation by modifying the older parts of the sapwood. As more cells are added under the bark, those in the deepest part of the sapwood die. The nutrients they contain are absorbed and replaced by various chemical substances called extractives (because they are easily removed with organic solvents). The modified wood is called heartwood (*see* Fig 3) and it is the various extractives that produce the odour, colour or durability that make timbers distinctive.

The lack of extractives means that sapwood cannot have durability, but this does not matter in the living tree because the sapwood cells are mostly saturated and do not contain much air. The presence of living cells that control metabolism in the sapwood also means the tree can respond to an invading pathogen by forming walls around it using resins, phenolic chemicals and other substances, depending on the type of tree. The dead heartwood that forms the majority of the trunk relies on deposited extractives for its defence, and it is this natural defence system that we exploit in converted timber. Trees that have a living strategy of deep roots and slow growth, such as oak, tend to have much more durable heartwood than trees that favour rapid dispersal and growth, such as birch.

Fig 3

Cambium produces sapwood cells. When the inner sapwood cells die (junction of yellow and black arrows) they become heartwood. It is only the heartwood that has natural durability.

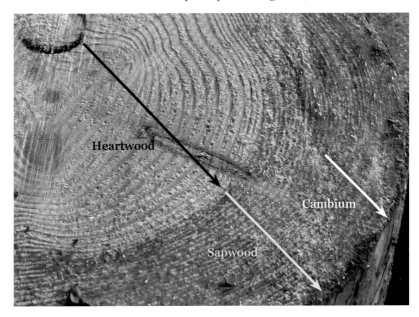

3

Eventually vigorous growth slows and the tree becomes senile. Increase in trunk height ceases first; increase in trunk diameter may continue for many years. Growth rings become narrow, and production of latewood (wood produced later in the year) declines. Latewood is stronger than early wood as the cell walls are much thicker, so a decline in latewood production means the wood becomes brittle. Changes in the heartwood then progress outwards from the pith (centre). These include the breakdown of extractives and the formation of minute compression fractures. Fungi invade via dead roots and eventually the tree becomes hollow.

When the tree is felled, the sapwood, which was protective in the living tree, dies and dries out. It is rapidly colonised by insects or fungi because it has no durability (Fig 4). The heartwood of durable timbers such as oak may resist decay for many years, even on the forest floor.

Moulds that consume the starch in newly felled sapwood are called blue-stain fungi. The colour is caused by the fungus spores and the wood is permanently stained. It has not, however, lost strength and can be used, provided that the appearance is not important.

The cross-sectional area of sapwood tends to stay constant up the tree, so the proportion of sapwood to heartwood will depend on the age and therefore thickness of the portion of trunk or branch. The age at which heartwood starts to form is quite variable, but around 20 years is common.

Logs are sawn to make building timbers and the distribution of the sapwood on each individual timber will depend on how the log is cut (Fig 5). These timbers will be used for building components and the distribution of the sapwood within the building will become random (Fig 6).

Fig 4

The sapwood of these felled pine logs has been attacked by moulds that consume the starch, followed by a wood-rotting fungus. The durable heartwood remains sound.

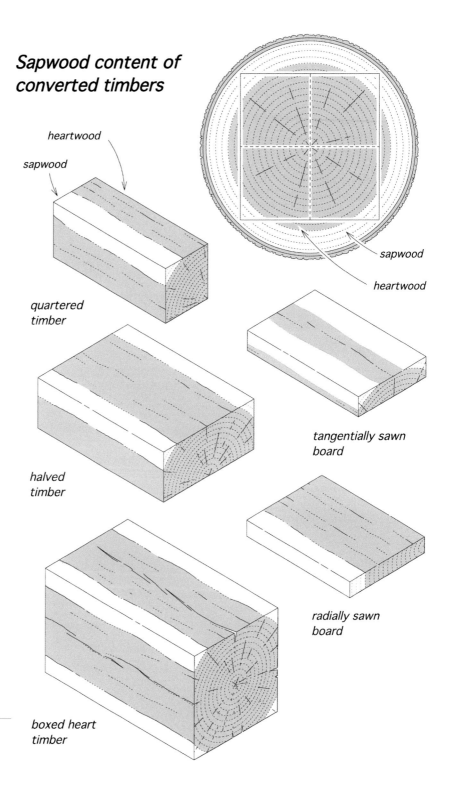

Sapwood content of converted timbers

heartwood

sapwood

sapwood

heartwood

quartered
timber

halved
timber

tangentially sawn
board

radially sawn
board

boxed heart
timber

Fig 5
Sapwood content of converted
timbers.

Fig 6

The distribution of the paler sapwood in this modern oak roof is random because of the way the timbers were cut and installed (some of the sapwood is indicated by arrows).

If a building remains dry then only the sapwood may be attacked by wood-boring insects and the attack will be limited. The random distribution of the sapwood may, however, give the impression that the infestation is widespread and that all of the timbers are at risk unless treated. Wide sapwood is common in plantation-grown softwoods because of their young age and narrow diameter when felled (*see* section 1.1.3). Oak sapwood in very old buildings has generally already been damaged or destroyed.

1.1.3 Durability and building timbers – a brief history

Prior to the 18th century most of the structural timbers that were used in UK buildings (at least those that have survived) and ships were oak. But as that century progressed, oak became very expensive and economics, together with other factors like fires in major cities and probably fashion, accelerated a change away from timber-frame construction and from the use of oak for structural components. Softwoods began to be used in large quantities.

English builders had been importing pine (often called fir) from Norway for centuries but this was mostly as planks. By the 18th century, softwoods were being used for structural timbers in situations previously reserved for oak. During the middle years of the 18th century the great European pine forests that could supply the Baltic ports began to be exploited. These forests could supply timber of dimensions that Norway no longer found easy to provide.

Timber had always been difficult to ship profitably because it was too bulky compared to its weight, and it tended to be imported as part of a cargo. Now the trade became sufficiently profitable and well organised to dedicate ships solely to timber importation.

The pinewood used during the 18th and 19th centuries was not as durable as oak, perhaps, but it resisted decay rather well. The reason was that the trees had grown for centuries in the natural woodlands of northern Europe and were mostly mature heartwood. The 20 or so years of sapwood growth on a 200- to 300-year-old tree formed an insignificant percentage of most logs (Fig 7).

Unfortunately, 200- to 300-year-old trees were not a sustainable resource, and by the First World War the wood was coming increasingly from regenerated forests.

Limited timber availability during the First World War caused considerable problems and when the war ended the UK government was determined never to be caught short of timber again. The government set up the Forestry Commission in 1919 to establish and manage large plantations of mainly softwood trees. This form of production became commonplace and necessary to sustain our growing demand for wood. The shift from wild forest to regenerated forest and plantations is now being replicated on a global scale. The consequences for biodiversity,

Fig 7

Section of plate from a Victorian church in Liverpool. The annual growth rings (one light early wood and one dark latewood) are so close together (because of the short growing season in northern Europe) that they are barely distinguishable. There are around 200 heartwood growth rings and the few sapwood rings on the corners were eroded by furniture beetle many years ago.

carbon dioxide absorption and a host of similar issues are hotly debated. The consequences for building conservation are not – even though we now have a century of experience of their performance.

The problem with growing trees as a managed crop is that they are felled as soon as they reach a marketable size. This is likely to be after about 50 years' growth as far as pine is concerned. Now the 20 or more years of sapwood growth become significant and the problem is compounded by the sale of younger 'thinnings' as the trees are given more space to grow. The result is that some sections of softwood now used for construction and repair may contain more than 50 per cent sapwood and are therefore inherently perishable. Trees could be grown for longer to develop more durable heartwood, but there is no commercial incentive to leave woodlands for long enough (Fig 8).

Because of its high sapwood content, much of the pinewood used in Britain since the First World War will not give the same durability in service as its historical equivalent, even though it is cut from the same species of tree. The sapwood may be easily destroyed by organisms such as furniture beetle and dry rot (see Fig 61) if the environment allows. Therefore old softwood timbers should be conserved wherever practical, not only because of their historical value, but also because they have a natural durability that cannot now be replicated. In contrast, oak felled today is generally as durable as historical oak.

Fig 8

These two sections of pine tree (*Pinus sylvestris*) both contain 200 years of growth. The small section came from Kenozero in north-west Russia, where the growing season is short. The large section grew as a park tree at Hagley Hall, Worcestershire, in the UK. The heartwood of both would have a similar durability. Bigger trees could be grown more rapidly in the UK than in northern Europe if it were economically viable. The Hagley tree was over-mature and starting to decay at its centre – an optimum age for pine conservation timbers in the UK and Ireland would probably be 80 to 100 years, but forest is rarely set aside for that length of time.

1.2 Decay and insect damage

Trees are converted into building timbers. Heartwood remains durable, but once the sapwood dries it has no natural protection against decay fungi or wood-boring insects. Nevertheless, decay is not inevitable and there are questions that should be asked when damaged timber is found and remedial action is contemplated. These include the following:

- What organism has caused the damage?
- Why is the problem there?
- How much damage has been caused?
- Is the decay or infestation current or historical?
- Will a targeted biocide treatment serve any useful purpose?

Let us examine each of the questions we should ask.

1.2.1 What organism has caused the damage?

Decay organisms will be discussed in parts 2 and 3, but it is appropriate to note here that this question should be approached with caution. This is because it can produce a set response that may not be appropriate to the particular situation. For example, it is generally assumed in the UK that dry rot will always require extensive treatment, while wet rot (decay caused by any other fungus, *see* Part 2) is easier to control. Dry rot, however, may be dead or unable to cause much damage, while a wet rot may be causing extensive decay. Contrary to perceived wisdom, strand-forming wet rots will travel through walls (though rarely to the extent that dry rot does) but because this is not supposed to happen the strands are either not noticed or the fungus is called dry rot. Calling the fungus dry rot will inevitably lead to an intervention that may be out of all proportion to the problem.

Similarly, the finding of a deathwatch beetle in a church might result in an expensive treatment when all that is required is the repair of a section of pew plinth against a damp wall.

1.2.2 Why is the problem there?

The predominant answer to this question is prolonged damp conditions. All of the fungi and insects that damage timbers in European buildings belong in the woodlands outside. They are all part of a decay cycle that takes a dead branch to the forest floor, breaks it down into soil and recycles the released nutrients back into trees. The breakdown of wood in this cycle creates environments for a progression of organisms to exploit, and if we allow our building timbers to replicate any one of these environments then the appropriate organism may cause damage. A poorly maintained roof is, after all, just a heap of damp, dead wood to a fungus. The moisture requirements for these decay organisms do vary a little and it is useful to look at their niches in the decay cycle to understand why. (Niche, in this context, is the part of the decay process – from tree to forest soil – that the organism has become adapted to exploit.)

None of the organisms that cause problems for timber conservation have adapted to a life in buildings and we must not expect them to tolerate conditions in buildings that they could not cope with in their forest environment. Buildings may provide a sheltered habitat that is ideal for some fungi (dry rot and the wet rots *Asterostroma* and *Donkioporia* are rarely found outside) but the same restrictions still apply. So what are these restrictions?

The decay cycle in a forest is caused by a progression of organisms. Dead branches on standing trees (Fig 9) provide a good starting point. Dead branches are an interesting habitat that may be damp or dry for extended periods of time. The organisms of interest to conservation from this environment are the anobiid beetles – furniture beetles (woodworm) and deathwatch beetles. (These are collectively and confusingly called powderpost beetles in the USA, whereas in the UK powderpost refers to the various species of *Lyctus*.)

Their natural environment (the dead parts of standing trees) gives them the ability to tolerate rather dry conditions (some genera better than others) but not without consequences if dry conditions are extended throughout the year. Evidence suggests that drying the timber prolongs the larval growth period, which produces smaller adults that lay fewer eggs. If the wood moisture content stays permanently below 15 per cent (which would be typical for a dry and well-maintained building in the UK), the beetles are not likely to re-infest building timbers and an existing population is likely to decline. It is possible that particularly nutritional wood might offset this decline to some extent. If the wood moisture content drops below about 10 per cent then the eggs and small larvae will desiccate. A significant insect infestation is therefore likely only if the timber remains damp.

The beetle larvae will attack only the sapwood of our commonly used construction timbers (pine and oak) because the heartwood contains a variety of substances that formed part of the tree's natural defence system against

Fig 9

The dead parts of standing trees provide a habitat for furniture beetle and deathwatch beetle. They can attack the dry sapwood and the heartwood that has been modified by fungus (*see* section 3.1) but they cannot spread into the saturated sapwood and unmodified heartwood of the living tree.

pathogens (Fig 10), as discussed in section 1.1.2. This is why the beetles do not move from a dead branch into the remainder of the tree. However, within the dead branch there will be decay and the fungus both softens the wood and changes its chemistry. This combination makes once-durable heartwood available to beetles that would otherwise be restricted to sapwood. The same effect is observed in buildings around the world (Fig 11). A little fungus denatures wall plates or the ends of traditionally durable building timbers and makes them susceptible to beetles and termites (Fig 12). Our task is to recognise

Fig 10 (right)
Old sapwood damage in a tie beam. The shape of the damage is typical of sapwood distribution – particularly the curved edges and the pointed end of the pale area. This pale area is historical damage and the sapwood has been eroded. The beetles cannot cause any further destruction in the unmodified heartwood and chemical treatment would serve no useful purpose.

Fig 11
The lower edge of this old oak panel has been decayed because the base of the wall was wet. There has been some secondary beetle infestation but the insects could not attack the remainder of the unmodified heartwood. Active infestation (if there still is any) will be removed with the repair. Treatment is not necessary, provided that the damp problem is resolved.

Fig 12
These old teak gates are in Amritsar, India. The bases seemed to be decaying and replacements were thought to be necessary. However, the gates are set above the marble floor so they must stay dry and decay is impossible. Enquiries revealed they had previously stood against a monastery wall for centuries. The damage was old and neither replacement nor treatment was necessary.

what has happened so that we don't treat a large amount of unmodified heartwood that the insects cannot attack. Frequently the repairs will remove the infestation without need for treatment.

When a branch falls to the forest floor it becomes wetter and the next group of insects and fungi take over. Durable timbers will take longer to decay than non-durable timbers, but all will eventually be destroyed. Fungus commences to attack when free water accumulates on and within the wood and the fungus spores absorb water, swell and rupture. This occurs at 'fibre saturation', which is the point at which no more water can attach to the cell walls, so that free water begins to accumulate. Fibre saturation in wood generally occurs at about 28 per cent moisture content (water compared with dry weight).

Wood gains or loses water molecules depending on the relative humidity (the amount of water the air is holding at a particular temperature as a percentage of the water it would contain at that temperature if saturated). High humidities donate water to the wood, while low humidities remove it. Temperature makes little difference to the wood moisture content, although it might affect the speed of response to change. This relationship between relative humidity and wood moisture content is called equilibration and resulting moisture contents, together with their consequences, are shown in Fig 13.

In practice, relative humidity is likely to fluctuate much faster than the wood will respond and so wood moisture contents may provide only an indication of the average relative humidity. The first few millimetres at the surface of the timber might respond in a day but moisture contents deeper in the wood might require weeks to change, and then variation might be small.

This equilibration has important consequences for an incautious surveyor with a moisture meter in an unheated building. The humidity in a dry but very cold roof might be high because relative humidity at any particular air moisture content rises as temperature drops. A survey in winter might, therefore, suggest that the roof timbers were wet enough for insects to attack. A survey of the same timbers in summer, however, when elevated temperatures lower the relative humidity, might

Fig 13

Equilibrium moisture contents at different relative humidities.

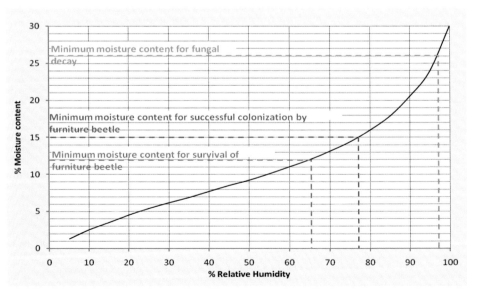

produce the opposite conclusion. The only way to overcome this problem is to use a resistance-type moisture meter fitted with electrodes insulated except at the tip. This will allow readings to be taken beneath the surface of the wood.

Relative humidity in a normal domestic environment would probably be between about 40 and 60 per cent. Figure 13 shows that this would produce equilibrium moisture contents of 8 to 12 per cent. Few decay organisms can cope with such low moisture contents and problems will occur only where there is some sustained source of water penetration.

A decay fungus (once the spore has germinated) might grow feebly onto wood with a moisture content as low as about 22 per cent but there will not be much damage until the wood is wetter. Remember that timber in a dry building will have a moisture content below about 15 per cent and decay can continue only if the wood remains wet. An accidental flooding cannot cause decay provided that the structure is dried. Forget silly stories about dry rot producing sufficient water from the breakdown of wood to survive in a dry building – it doesn't happen (*see* section 2.5.1). If timber becomes wet and remains wet for some reason (Figs 14 and 15) then it will decay. If the water is removed, then the fungus must die.

The insects that feed on rotting logs in a forest include weevils and there are several species that we might find in an equivalent habitat within European buildings. An equivalent habitat in this case might be a damp wall plate under a suspended ground floor. The weevil/fungus combination will destroy the plate unless it dries, in which case the fungus will die and the weevils will fly away. The heartwood remains denatured, however, and might potentially form a future food source for furniture beetle or deathwatch beetle.

The only wood-feeding insect that might tolerate lower moisture contents for much of its life cycle would probably be the powderpost beetle (*see* section 3.2.2). These beetles live on starch in freshly cut timber and the breakdown of starch into individual glucose molecules releases water within the insect's digestive system. Powderpost beetles, however, produce a transient infestation because they die out when the starch level within the sapwood drops.

Some other beetles, particularly the longhorn beetles (*see* section 3.2.1), may emerge from timber long after it is installed within a building if the larva was large enough to avoid desiccation when the wood dried. Low moisture contents prolong the growth period and beetles have been found to emerge perhaps 20 years after timber was installed or furniture was brought into a

Fig 14 (below)
Infill panels have been replaced with brick and hard cement render. The cement panels have shrunk away from the timber, allowing water to become trapped behind them and causing the frame to decay. Extensive repairs are necessary.

Fig 15 (below right)
This purlin end has decayed because it was embedded in a wall that remained wet because of a roof fault.

building. Items made from tropical hardwoods can produce some unusual insects after several years with no signs of infestation. However, these insects cannot re-infest (eggs and newly hatched larvae have no resistance to desiccation and beetles would not choose to lay their eggs in dry wood).

1.2.3 How much damage has been caused?

Establishing the extent of decay requires careful inspection. Decay fungi change the nature of the timber so that it no longer has the characteristics of sound wood. Decayed wood becomes brittle (Fig 16).

Brown-rot fungi (*see* section 2.2) will cause timber to fracture into cubes by differential shrinkage but this will not occur until the timber dries (Figs 17 and 18).

Concealed damage may not be found during a survey but may become apparent when building works have been completed – particularly if the room is heated and the relative humidity drops to a low level. Once shrinkage starts, the drying process accelerates, leading to the erroneous conclusion that the fungus is spreading rapidly and that it does not require water.

Small cracks or unevenness may be the first indication of decay (Fig 19) and any surface distortion should be investigated for softness with a small screwdriver or similar probe. If there is active decay then the source of moisture must be located and eliminated. If the decay is active then the timber will crack much more as it dries.

Fig 16

Sample 1 (top) is sound wood that splinters as it breaks. Sample 2 (bottom) is decayed and snaps without splinters. This makes a useful test for decay in small samples.

Fig 17 (above)
The back of this skirting board is partially decayed but it keeps its shape because it is wet.

Fig 18 (above right)
Distortion during drying can lead to the erroneous conclusion that dry rot is still alive and growing rapidly, even though the source of water has been removed. This photograph shows a door case that cracked within a year or two of building restoration, the delay being the time it took for the thick wall to dry.

As discussed earlier, wood-boring insects will attack the sapwood of normal construction timbers only if they become damp (moisture content greater than about 15 per cent). The heartwood will be attacked only if its chemistry has been modified by fungus.

This means that a small amount of old sapwood damage caused by furniture beetle in a Victorian softwood roof (for example) certainly does not mean that all the timbers could become infested, even if the infestation is still active (which it generally isn't). The amount of sapwood present will depend on the age of the timber and how it was cut, but the amount in a Victorian or Edwardian roof is going to be very limited, although randomly distributed. Spraying with an insecticide would mostly treat timbers that the beetles could never attack. The best treatment is to ensure that the roof remains dry.

Fig 19
Cracks and surface distortions demonstrate partial drying during active decay. Any change to the surface of the timber should be investigated with a probe to see if the timber under the paint layer is soft.

1.2.4 Is the decay or infestation current or historical?

If insect infestation is current then there will be dead beetles present on the floor or on windowsills where they have flown towards the light (Fig 20). The appearance of the damage can be entirely misleading. If current activity is suspected then tissue paper or card can be tightly fastened over groups of holes (*see* section 3.1.2.2). If beetles emerge they will bite an exit hole, thus demonstrating their presence.

Decay fungi will be alive only if the wood is wet and even then the fungus may be dead and caused by some earlier event. Much of the dry rot and other rots treated in buildings may have been dead for decades. Most old buildings would be found to have some decay after a century or two of variable

Fig 20

If a beetle infestation is active then the presence of dead beetles will be a more reliable indicator than the appearance of the damage. Windowsills, ledges, edges of carpets and spiders' webs are all good places to look. Some of the beetles in this photograph are wrapped in spider's web.

maintenance if all the timbers were exposed (Fig 21). Dead decay might require repair, but it does not require treatment.

One method of determining if the wood and fungus is damp is to place fragments in a polythene bag and leave it somewhere warm. If condensation forms, there will probably be enough water to sustain fungus. Dry-rot strands also become brittle when they dry because of their cellulose-like chitin content (chitin is the material that gives insect shells (exoskeletons) their rigidity). Any live dry-rot strand will remain flexible, as will those of strand-producing wet-rot fungi.

1.2.5 Will a targeted biocide treatment serve any useful purpose?

Scientific and popular opinion has veered sharply away from the indiscriminate use of chemicals, as exemplified by the old remedial-industry expression 'belt and braces treatment'. The analogy was to a pair of trousers. If both a belt and braces were used, the trousers should not fall down. Similarly, if all that the chemical industry had to offer was poured onto dry rot and injected into the walls then something should kill the fungus.

Nowadays the realisation that the application of biocides can have unanticipated consequences, particularly in agriculture, is resulting in a change of approach to pest control. This change is called Integrated Pest Management (IPM) or Integrated Pest Control (IPC). These concepts fit well with conservation, and also with our slowly growing awareness that if we are to remain living on this planet we had better take greater care of it. Many people do not want biocides sprayed or injected into their houses, no matter how low the hazard rating claimed by the manufacturer.

An integrated approach to pest management or control is one that takes account of the targeted organism's natural requirements and biology so that

Fig 21

If dry rot and other fungi are dry then they are dead. If there is any remnant of live fungus because the source of water has only just been removed, then it can be reactivated only by a significant and sustained source of water. The church lintel shown in this photograph was damaged years before. It requires replacement but the wall does not require treatment, despite remnants of dry rot.

biocides form only a part of the control strategy. Biocides are used only where there is a specific requirement for them, and then in the minimum quantity necessary to accomplish the task.

If an insect infestation can be shown to be active (not necessarily by the appearance of the damage, as Fig 22 shows) and sufficient of the timber can be accessed, then treatment with an appropriate biocide would be justifiable. However, treatment should, wherever practical, form part of works to remove the conditions that allowed the infestation to develop.

Treatment for fungi is more difficult to justify because they are easier to kill, but carefully targeted biocide application may help to contain a problem while a structure dries.

In both cases chemical treatments should form part of a remedial strategy and not the automatic response. It is important not to cause more damage than the organism you seek to control.

In the pest management world, our experience with modern timbers in modern buildings has coloured our approach to historic timbers. Dry rot and furniture beetle will cause damage at a rate and to an extent in 20th-century, plantation-grown wood that would be impossible in the wild-grown historical equivalents. Unfortunately our perception and response to the two situations is frequently the same, to the detriment of the building, its finishes and our living environment.

Fig 22

Dust trails in this softwood roof at Lincoln Cathedral had led to the conclusion on several occasions that there was current furniture beetle infestation. We first saw this in 1996 and again in 2006, when nothing had changed. On neither occasion were there any beetles. These are old frass trails (faecal pellets and wood dust) from thin residual sapwood; the dust has not been dislodged and the infestation is historic.

2 | Wood-destroying fungi

2.1 Decay fungi and their requirements

2.1.1 Types of decay

The decay of timber presents organisms with a complex problem. Some can only live on cell contents because they have little ability to digest the cell wall. Moulds and stain fungi, for example, usually cause little damage, although they may cause discolouration of damp timber. They do, however, have a part to play in the natural cycle of decay by increasing porosity and detoxifying some natural fungicides. Timber-decay fungi cause three forms of decay (soft rot, brown rot and white rot), depending on their ability to attack the three structural molecules (Fig 23) that make up wood (glucose, lignin and hemicellulose).

- **Soft rots**: These cause surface decay in very wet timbers and timbers that are periodically wetted. They principally attack cellulose and hemicelluloses. The fungus produces distinctive cavities within the cell wall because the fungal enzymes, which cause decomposition, do not diffuse far from the fungal tip. The result is a fine cuboidal checking of the surface when the timber dries (Fig 24). These fungi cause only superficial decay in temperate climates, but can cause significant damage where climates are too hot or too cold for other fungi to flourish. Significant rot damage is more common in timbers exposed to soil or aquatic environments than it is in buildings. The characteristic cubed appearance is, however, sometimes visible on interior timbers (Fig 25), demonstrating that these were once exposed on the exterior of a building and have been reused.

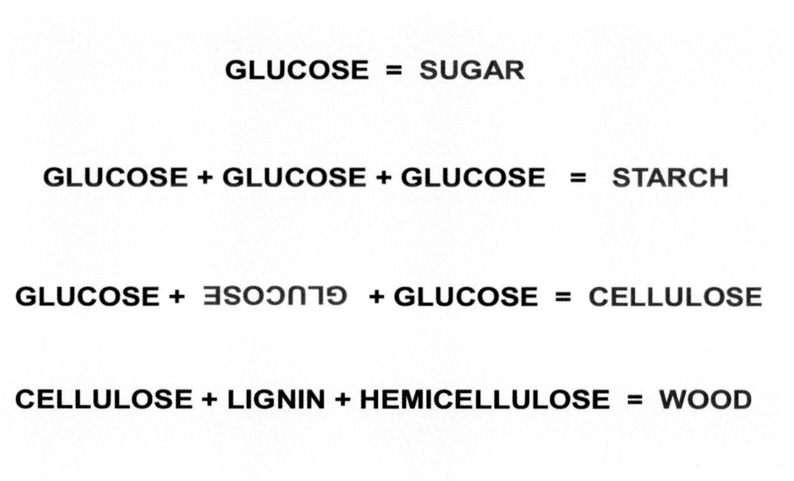

Fig 23

Photosynthesis produces glucose. Glucose molecules are capable of linking together to form starch, which is a polymer that is easily broken down again as an energy resource. If alternate molecules are inverted (shown in red in this figure) then cellulose is constructed. This forms stable, long chains that provide strength within the wood cell wall. The small cellulose fibres are surrounded by shorter branched sugar molecules called hemicelluloses, which provide elasticity, and both are embedded in a matrix of lignin that resists compression and allows the tree to grow tall. Lignins are immensely complicated, but based on different combinations of only three phenolic molecules.

GLUCOSE = SUGAR

GLUCOSE + GLUCOSE + GLUCOSE = STARCH

GLUCOSE + ƎSOƆU˥⅁ + GLUCOSE = CELLULOSE

CELLULOSE + LIGNIN + HEMICELLULOSE = WOOD

Fig 25
This ceiling beam is in the front room of a house in Suffolk, but the fine surface soft-rot damage suggests that it was once an exterior timber, perhaps part of a house frame or a barn. Good timbers were reused when a building fell into disrepair.

Fig 24
Surface checking on this timber is caused by soft rot. This is a form of surface damage caused by moulds and some other small fungi that create cavities parallel to the cellulose fibres in the cell wall, predominantly of hardwoods. Soft rots are found in timbers that are wet or intermittently wetted. The fine surface checking forms as the surface dries.

- **Brown rots:** Decay caused by these fungi may penetrate deep within the timber, sometimes leaving a sound outer skin of wood. The fungi are able to destroy the cellulose and hemicelluloses (as in soft rots) but the lignin is only modified. Hemicellulose is broken down first, producing hydrogen peroxide, which is able to penetrate deep into the timber, breaking down the cellulose. The fragile brown matrix of lignin that the fungus leaves cracks into cubes by differential shrinkage as it dries (Figs 26 and 27). These fungi may cause considerable damage, particularly to softwoods. Typical examples would be cellar rot and dry rot.

Fig 26
Brown rots remove the cellulose and hemicelluloses, leaving a fragile matrix of brown lignin, which cracks into cubes as it dries. There is a rapid and drastic loss in strength. Weight loss may eventually exceed 70 per cent.

Fig 27
Brown rots are frequently found in embedded bearings if the wall has been damp for a prolonged time.

- **White rots:** Fungi that cause this type of damage are able to attack lignin and some destroy most of the constituents of the wood. All that is left is a spongy fibrous mass of white cellulose (Figs 28 and 29). White rots seem to require more water than brown rots and they tend to be more common in hardwoods than in softwoods.

Fig 28

In this photograph, a white rot has decayed the plate and hip rafter ends of a roof. Some species of white-rotting fungi preferentially attack hemicellulose and lignin, while others attack all cell components at the same rate. Weight loss may eventually exceed 95 per cent.

Fig 29

A typical example of white-rot damage. White rots seem to prefer hardwoods because they have difficulty breaking down the phenolic unit that predominates in softwood lignin.

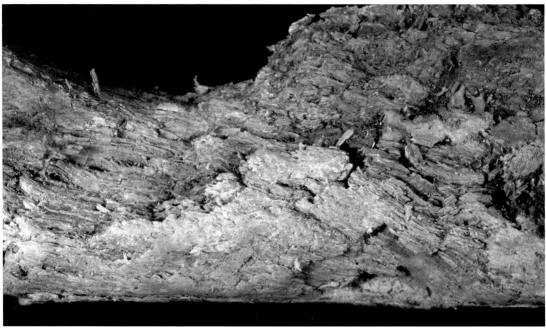

The fungi that will mostly decay branches or logs on the forest floor are saprophytes. Their niche in nature is the breakdown of dead organic materials, and it is these saprophytes that cause the majority of the damage to building timbers (termites may be a far greater problem in drier climates).

There are many different types of saprophytic fungi in woodland and if one cannot grow well on the log there will always be another that can. Even the most durable of woods is slowly consumed by a progression of organisms in a damp environment, although this may take a very long time.

2.1.2 Wet rot, dry rot and mythology

The differentiation between dry rot and wet rot has probably caused more misconceptions and unnecessary destruction in historic buildings than any other misunderstanding in conservation. The roots of the problem go back to 18th-century England, when the massive change in usage from oak to pine (*see* section 1.1.3) had unforeseen consequences. There would not have been a serious decay problem if the properties of the pine had been better understood. Unfortunately, pine was frequently seen just as a lighter and cheaper alternative to oak and the connection between decay and moist environments was not made. Pine was used for the upper works of dank ships, or embedded in the damp floors of houses, and the consequence was an epidemic of 'dry rot'. At least seven books and pamphlets were published on the subject in the UK during the first three decades of the 19th century.

The damage was called dry rot because people didn't understand that the problem was connected with water. The damage they were used to in oak they believed to be caused by wind and rain and they called it wet or common rot, but this new form seemed frequently to occur behind a sound skin of timber (Fig 30). This, together with the friable lignin matrix that remained, caused our

Fig 30
Brown-rot fungi often keep a sound outer skin of timber (*see* arrow). This led people to believe in the 18th and early 19th centuries that decay was caused by internal fermentation rather than water. The damage was called dry rot. White rot (*see* Fig 29) seems to progress from the outside inwards and was thought to be caused by wind and water. This decay was called wet rot or common rot.

ancestors to deduce that they were dealing with a new form of decay caused by the fermentation of sap and vital forces within the timber. They called it dry rot because (to them) it was clearly not caused by water. Those, like the English botanist James Sowerby, who were familiar with the flora of woodlands had no difficulty in understanding what was going on, but they were not generally believed. One popular theory was that the damage was caused by a fluctuation of heat, and its true cause was not finally accepted until the 1860s.

We now know that their 'dry rots' were caused by brown-rot fungi and their 'wet rots' by white-rot fungi. But the term dry rot still leads to confusion today. Brown rots were not a new phenomenon, but they were thrown into public awareness by the change in timber usage.

The dry-rot controversy had been resolved by the end of the 19th century and the causes of the decay were understood. If you found dry rot then you repaired the damage and removed the source of water. This was not a new concept really because a man called J Johnson had written a book on the subject in 1795. The definition of dry rot was also changing and had become restricted to those fungi that produced plenty of surface growth. The remainder of the brown-rotting fungi were relegated to the wet rots.

Unfortunately the 18th- and early 19th-century distinction between wet rot and dry rot has stayed with us, and the term 'dry' still leads many people to conclude that the fungus does not require much water. Some of the problem is that dry-rot growth can look white and fluffy even when it's dead; and concealed damage can deform rapidly as it desiccates. Both phenomena lead to the conclusion that the dry rot is active, even though the source of moisture may be long gone (*see* Fig 18).

So originally the concept of dry rot included all brown-rotting fungi. By the 20th century it had been restricted to those brown-rot fungi that produced extensive strand growth and it was not restricted to the single fungus *Serpula lacrymans* until a British Standard of 1963. All of the remaining significant decay fungi – brown rots and white rots – were then lumped together as wet rots.

2.2 Fungi that cause brown rots

There are a large number of woodland fungi that might find their way into damp buildings. There is little purpose in attempting a list of all of them here and in most cases their identity is not important. A few are sufficiently common or important to warrant some comment.

2.2.1 Dry rot (*Serpula lacrymans*)
Dry rot appears to be rather uncommon in woodland habitats, but it can thrive in buildings if conditions allow. This may be in part because a damp building provides a sheltered environment, but there is also evidence to indicate that the fungus needs calcium and iron – two elements that are very common in building materials. These requirements probably explain why the fungus is usually associated with timbers in contact with walls or ceiling plaster.

Dry rot is usually associated with softwoods in buildings, although it will attack less durable hardwoods. The practical consequences are that, while the fungus might grow over oak joists or panelling from softwood board or fixings, it will rarely cause much damage, and treatment of the oak once the fungus has been scraped off is not really necessary. Certainly there is no reason to discard or cut back the oak.

The fresh dry-rot fruit is usually dark orange in colour with a white margin and a cratered/folded spore-producing surface (Fig 31). The spores, which are analogous to seeds, are released in huge quantities and may produce a distinctive fine, brown, talc-like dust layer on surfaces (Fig 32). Once the spores are

Fig 31

This photograph shows dry-rot fruits in a subfloor void, where the floor-joist ends have decayed. The inset shows the distinctive surface-sculpturing of the fruit.

Fig 32

The minute dry-rot spores are brown and are produced in such enormous quantities that they have the capacity to cover all available surfaces, as is shown here. A dry-rot fruit measuring 1 sq m has been calculated to produce 500 million spores in 10 minutes. Spore viability is, however, very low and few spores are capable of germination.

released, the fruit shrivels and darkens (Fig 33), but the surface sculpture still remains discernible.

Spores may germinate if there is free water on the surface or within the timber, and this generally implies a timber moisture content of 28 to 30 per cent. The little threads of fungus (hyphae) produced by spore germination are microscopic, but they tend to clump together and form a variety of surface growths called mycelia (Figs 34–37).

One form of mycelium is the strand, which has an ability to penetrate masonry and grow over inert surfaces (*see* Fig 37). The presence of this type of mycelium is said to indicate dry rot, but many strand-producing fungi can grow within walls if conditions are suitable. The purpose of the strand is to conduct the products of timber digestion around the fungus. It is not to convey water in order to moisten dry timber, and any wetting effect is very restricted. Except under exceptional circumstances, active dry rot does not spread far from the zone of wetting.

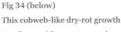

Fig 33 (right)

The brown dry-rot fruit turns black when all the spores have been released (as shown in this photograph) but the outline of the distinctive sculpturing (*see* Fig 31) is usually still visible.

Fig 34 (below)

This cobweb-like dry-rot growth in a floor void was easy to miss because the boards were thick and wet, so they had not distorted.

Fig 35 (below right)

Cotton wool-like growth was easily visible in the cellar below the floorboards shown in Fig 34 because the wall was wet and the surface relative humidity was above 90 per cent.

Fig 36

Considerable surface growth like the skin of a mushroom may also be produced by dry rot and yellow, burgundy or lilac patches may appear in response to stress factors such as light (*see* inset).

Fig 37

Dry rot produces strands which (like several other fungi) have the ability to penetrate cracks or soft mortar in walls and grow over inert surfaces. These strands are popularly supposed to carry water to moisten dry timber but their ability to do this is limited and no better than any other strand-producing fungus.

Dry rot, if vigorously active, may attack timber with a moisture content of about 22 per cent under laboratory conditions, but in practice not much activity is observed in buildings at timber moisture-content levels below about 24 per cent. Research suggests that the optimum moisture level in timber is probably between 30 and 70 per cent. There is no evidence whatsoever that buildings dry down through a stage which favours dry-rot growth. Dry rot, as noted earlier, is invariably associated with walls or plaster because it has a requirement for calcium, and both mortar and plaster are rich in that element. These building materials also tend to hold water and maintain a stable environment. Temperature also has a significant effect, and decay is optimum between 21 and 23°C. Growth ceases at about 0°C and above about 28°C.

The upper moisture limit is difficult to assess, but no fungus will survive if wood is saturated to the exclusion of air. I have, however, frequently seen dry rot growing vigorously on very wet floorboards with rainwater dripping through them. Excess moisture is lost as droplets from the surface when the air is saturated (Fig 38).

Growth rates for the fungus have been published and these are also sometimes needed to resolve disputes (for example, situations where the length of time the fungus has been growing is used to establish legal responsibility). It is important, however, not to confuse rates of growth with rates of decay. A reasonable estimate for growth would be 5 to 9mm per day or around 1.5m per year (there would not be much growth in winter). Rates might be lower in cold cellars.

Decay rates are also sometimes required in litigation and these are often based on a 10mm cube of sapwood. This provides a spurious conclusion because the surface area to volume ratio of a cube is considerably different to that of a beam end or joist. There are some published results that are more useful. The Building Research Establishment published weight losses from 100mm × 25mm × 12.5mm blocks of pine heartwood exposed to various fungi for four months. Dry rot caused an average weight loss of 6.75 per cent, which was less than the other fungi tested (Building Research Establishment 1972).

There is no doubt that dry rot growing in a wet and neglected building can cause a considerable amount of damage (Fig 39). But this takes time; it does not happen in a few weeks or usually even months. The wood must be damp and the dampness must continue or the fungus will die. A burst pipe that is found and remedied after a few days cannot set up some brooding fungus that will slowly decay the building and burst out in the years to come. Neither will dry rot caused by a blocked drain spread to devour the whole house. For every dry-rot outbreak that requires significant intervention there are very many that can easily be resolved if the situation is understood (Fig 40).

Dry rot can be a very difficult fungus to eradicate but this is not inevitable. Dry rot attacking modern softwood joinery in a damp basement, where the walls are impossible to dry, presents a very different problem to dry rot attacking a 19th-century floor-beam bearing behind a faulty downpipe at first-floor level, where the source of water can be removed. Exposure works and fungicidal treatments, which are perhaps relevant in the first case, may be unjustifiably destructive in the second. If a 'standard dry-rot treatment' is used, however, then it must inevitably be designed for the worst-case scenarios and may cause substantial unnecessary damage. Careful consideration of the specific outbreak, location and cause is needed before an approach is agreed.

Fig 38
Excess moisture is lost as droplets if the air is saturated with moisture. This phenomenon gives the dry-rot fungus its scientific name, *Serpula lacrymans* (*lacrymans* means 'weeping').

Fig 39 (above)
Dry rot in a neglected building can cause considerable damage, but only if the environment is wet and remains wet. This seems mostly to be because some strains of the fungus grow very vigorously rather than because of any special ability that separates dry rot from other decay fungi.

Fig 40 (right)
Dry rot had attacked the lining of this confessional in a Dublin church (a). When dry rot is discovered, the primary control measure is to locate and remove the source of water penetration, as the fungus will die when the source of water is removed. In this case, the water source was a blocked drain and a gap at the base of the wall (b).

The fungus may preferentially attack softwoods but the rate of decay varies significantly according to the timber. The fungus might easily destroy a piece of modern pine, full of sapwood, but struggle to cause any damage to a piece of 19th-century mature heartwood of the same tree species in the same timeframe (*see* Fig 61). A Baltic pine beam end embedded in a permanently wet wall might eventually be destroyed but the fungus could take years to accomplish this.

The treatment of dry rot is always more thorough than for wet rots, but dry rot does not necessarily cause significant damage, while strand-producing wet rots can cause substantial damage. Recommendations for treatment in this book are therefore based on the potential the fungus has to cause damage, rather than on its name. These recommendations are incorporated into Table 2.

2.2.2 Cellar rot (*Coniophora puteana*)

Cellar rot (Fig 41) is said to be the commonest wet rot found in buildings, where it will attack both softwoods and hardwoods. In practice, the name tends to be applied to any cubed decay with no particular diagnostic features. The accurate visual identification of a decay-causing fungus is usually impossible unless fruits are present, but the cubed damage caused by cellar rot is frequently blackened by the production of melanin. The strands are also dark and fan-like (Figs 42 and 43), and readily penetrate old mortar joints. Contrary to popular belief, cellar-rot fruits, which are olive-brown, bumpy and with a white margin, are fairly common in buildings. They tend, however, to be misidentified as dry rot, if they are recognised as a fruit at all. Misidentification is particularly likely when the fungus is causing extensive damage.

Cellar rot's environmental requirements do not differ significantly from dry rot. Brown rots generally seem to vary more in their temperature tolerance than they do in their moisture requirements.

Fig 41 (opposite)

Fruit of the cellar-rot fungus growing in the corner of a storeroom. The inset shows the lumpy, spore-producing surface, which is very different to that of dry rot, although the fruits are sometimes confused.

Fig 42

Cellar-rot growth can be quite extensive and strands easily penetrate walls. If there is significant damage then it is usually mistakenly considered to be dry rot. Cellar rot attacks both softwoods and hardwoods.

Fig 43 (above)

Cellar-rot mycelium is white when the spore generates but turns chocolate brown as it matures. Dry rot is never this colour unless it has been spray-treated.

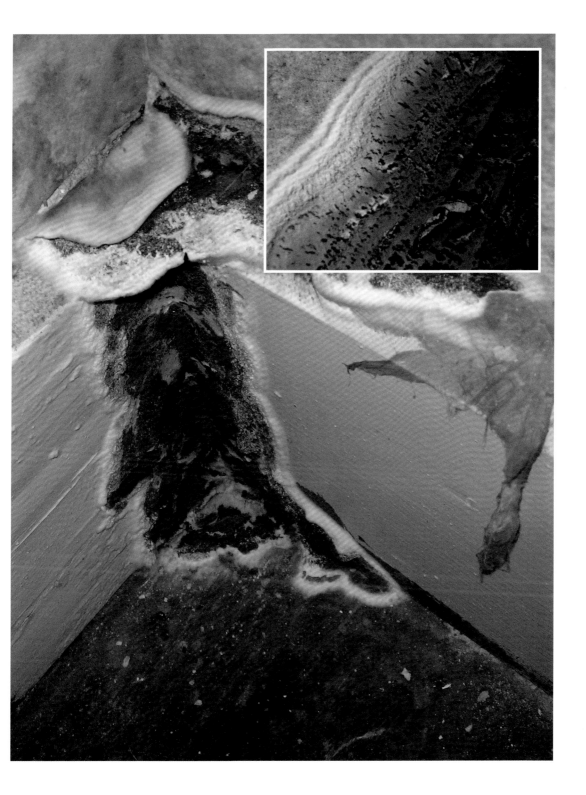

2.2.3 Mine fungus (*Antrodia viallantii*) and other pore fungi

The mine fungus (Fig 44) was given its common name by mycologists W P K Findlay and K St G Cartwright, who found it growing extensively on pit props. It is generally included as a building fungus, although in my experience it is not particularly common, at least in the UK. It is, however, a relevant example of a pore fungus. This group of fungi all produce spores in tubes that appear at the surface as pores of different shapes and sizes (Fig 45). Identification is a

Fig 44 (above)

The mine fungus is one of a large group of
woodland fungi that are commonly found in
buildings. Spores are produced in tubes, with the
top visible as a pore on the surface. Fruits found
in buildings are frequently misshapen but the
pores should still be visible, as shown in the inset.

Fig 45 (right)

A fruit of the pore fungus *Gloeophyllum
sepiarium*, showing a typical fruit form with the
characteristic pores. I have found this species
mostly in conservatory frames. Any lump of
fungus found in a building should be examined
for surface pores, but species identification rarely
provides more useful information.

specialist task, which rarely provides more useful information and so the fungi are easier to describe simply as 'pore fungi'. They are important in the woodland ecosystem and many different types are found decaying dead wood on the forest floor. Some of these will find their way into buildings, where they may cause brown rots or white rots, depending on the species.

Mycelium of the pore fungi found in buildings may be brilliant white or some shade of brown but does not have the same mushroom/white colour and growth pattern as dry rot (Figs 46 and 47).

Fig 46 (above)
Mycelium of mine fungus is brilliant white, an intensity rarely found in dry rot. The growth pattern tends to be more fern-like or feathery.

Fig 47 (right)
Mycelium of an unidentified pore fungus growing on the underside of floorboards in a cellar. These fungi generally need a considerable and sustained source of damp.

2.3 Fungi that cause white rots

2.3.1 Oak rot (*Donkioporia expansa*)

Donkioporia (Fig 48) and the closely related *Phellinus* species are serious causes of damage in buildings around the world. All are pore fungi, but the fruits are generally rather thick and firm and the pores are very small. The colour of the fruit is usually dark grey to brown/purple.

Two species, *Donkioporia expansa* and the closely related *Phellinus ferruginosus*, are a major cause of damage to oak building timbers. Both fungi will attack softwoods, but this does not seem to be common in the UK.

Donkioporia decay is usually concealed, and is generally discovered either by tapping the timber to find hollow sections or by finding the fruits, which are woody in appearance, and may be 200 to 300mm long. Fruits are perennial, eventually becoming rather thick and layered. *P. ferruginosus* also fruits readily in buildings, and may produce brown surface growth. *Donkioporia* does not usually develop mycelium in buildings, although it will in culture.

The minimum moisture content for oak-rot growth is about 23 to 25 per cent. The optimum and maximum moisture levels have not been established, but it certainly thrives where timber is visibly wet. This requirement for high moisture levels means that the oak-rot fungus may have caused extensive damage at the backs of plates or within truss bearings, for example, without any damage being apparent on the drier surface (Figs 49 and 50). However, fruits will generally be present and any lumpy growths should be checked for a pore structure. If concealed decay is suspected, the timber should be tapped – a hollow sound will indicate interior damage or damage at the back of the component.

Fig 48

The oak-rot fungus belongs to a group of fungi that are commonly found damaging heritage buildings in many countries. The fruits are generally thick and perennial, with very small pores, but distinctive tubes are revealed when the fruit is broken (*see* inset). Oak rot is an unusual fungus because it rarely produces normal (sexual) spores, and is rarely found away from worked timber.

Fig 49
There were no obvious signs of decay in this roof space but the plate sounded hollow when tapped.

Fig 50
The end of the truss shown in Fig 49, as exposed from outside the building by removing the parapet gutter. The bearing of the truss and the back of the plate have been severely damaged by oak rot and deathwatch beetle.

Growth occurs between 5 and 40°C, with an optimum temperature of about 25 to 30°C. The behaviour of cultures grown under laboratory conditions suggests that decay progresses slowly compared to some other oak-rotting fungi. Nevertheless, severe damage may be caused to plates, joints and bearings in time, and the fungus is frequently not discovered until decay is advanced.

Donkioporia is not found away from buildings in the UK but has been found in bridges and other man-made structures in Western Europe.

2.3.2 *Asterostroma cervicolor*

Asterostroma is an uncommon woodland fungus that has been collected from both deciduous and coniferous trees in north-western Europe. Like oak rot and dry rot, it seems to have found buildings to be a congenial environment, where it is one of the few white-rot fungi associated with softwood. It is discussed here because the fungus is commonly found, and because it produces surface growth that is frequently profuse, and usually readily identifiable.

The fruit (Fig 51) is flat and light brown, the same colour as the strands. The white-rot damage should alone be enough to differentiate this fungus from dry rot but there is frequently confusion.

The fungus produces large quantities of mycelium, ranging in colour from cinnamon to burgundy, and sometimes strands (Figs 52 and 53). Little has been reported regarding the moisture and temperature requirements of the fungus, but it may frequently be found in cellars and other locations where walls and embedded timbers are wet. Curiously, the extent of visible growth usually suggests far more damage than is found when decayed timber is located. Nevertheless, this is an important decay organism whose presence indicates conditions suitable for more virulent decay fungi.

Fig 51

Asterostroma is commonly found attacking softwoods in buildings. The fruit is light brown and there is no sculptured surface from which the spores are produces (*see* inset). Note that *Asterostroma* weeps like dry rot if there is plenty of water available.

Fig 52
Asterostroma usually produces large amounts of surface growth, which ranges in colour from cinnamon to burgundy.

Fig 53
Asterostroma strands might be mistaken for cellar rot, but they range in colour from cinnamon to burgundy rather than chocolate brown and there are usually more ginger areas present. These strands, like those of other strand-producing fungi, will grow through cracks in walls and are frequently mistaken for dry rot, with serious consequences. The quantity of surface growth is frequently much greater than the amount of decay.

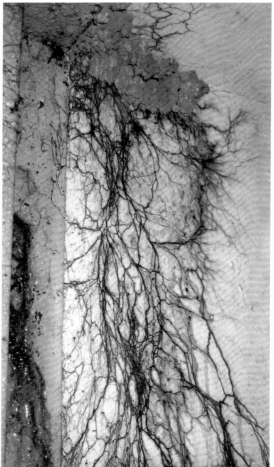

2.3.3 Ink cap (*Coprinus*)

These are gilled fungi (Fig 54) that are usually considered to cause minor decay to oak timbers. However, while damage to beams or lintels is usually minor, the fungi can cause more serious damage to ceiling or wall laths if the source of water is not checked. Damaged laths may distort when a building is restored and heated, leading to localised ceiling collapse.

The fruits are a traditional toadstool shape with slender stems and black gills. The cap liquefies as the spores are released, and eventually the fruit remains as a thread with a blob on the end. Ginger or golden-coloured growth (Fig 55) may be produced and the strands will grow extensively through walls.

Fig 54

The ink cap fungus starts as a gilled toadstool (*see* inset) but the cap liquefies as the spores are released until all that remains is a thread with a blob on the end. This is an indicator of possible concealed decay.

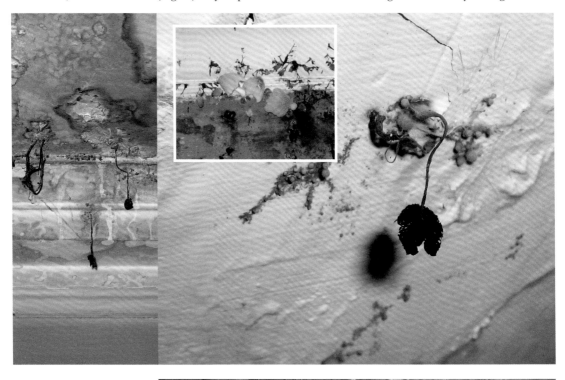

Fig 55

The mycelium of ink cap is golden brown, with strands that may be found in walls.

2.4 Fungi that indicate damp but do not cause decay

Fig 56

The cup fungus (*Peziza domeciliana*) is common in buildings, where it is an indicator of water penetration.

2.4.1 Cup fungus (*Peziza domiciliana*)

The cup fungus (*Peziza domeciliana*) is a saprophytic fungus that feeds on rotting wood and other organic debris (Fig 56). Spores are produced within the body of the fungus so there is no distinctive fertile surface. The fruit may be 100mm across, though most are smaller. Treatment is not required. Fig 57 shows an unidentified *Peziza*.

Fig 57
A large unidentified *Peziza*. These
fungi produce large amounts of
mould-like white surface growth,
as can be seen on the underside of
the ceiling (*see* inset).

2.5 The treatment of decay

2.5.1 The changing philosophy of decay treatment

A good starting point when considering the philosophy of wood-decay treatment in the 20th century would be Ernest G Blake, who produced a book entitled *Enemies of Timber* in 1925. Blake was apparently a 'Medallist in Sanitary Building Construction' and he wrote a series of books for building professionals. His chapters on dry rot are of interest because they indicate popular contemporary thought that had not changed much since the early 19th century.

His explanation for wet rot was that 'the intermittent action of air and water results in the oxidation of the lignin' and he believed that the actual wood breakdown was caused by bacteria. He seems to have assumed this in situations where there was brown-rot damage but no significant visible fungus growth.

Dry rot, according to Blake, was a 'plant parasite' that when it reached maturity assumed the form of a fungus. This would presumably be when the strands (which he calls 'roots') appear. He recognised three major forms of dry rot (modern-day dry rot, cellar rot and mine fungus), of which modern-day dry rot (*Serpula lacrymans*) was the most virulent because, Blake believed, it could sustain itself on water from the breakdown of wood in a dry environment. This was a curious but widespread belief. However, if a fungus breaks down a quantity of wood, the wood will produce the same quantity of water irrespective of which fungus caused the decomposition. Dry rot cannot somehow squeeze more water out.

After an extraordinarily muddled section on fungus biology, Blake concluded with a dire warning: 'Even if it is the least harmful species of dry rot, no quarter must be given as none will be received, and it would only be courting disaster to adopt half-hearted measures at such a critical time' (Blake 1925, 46).

It is no surprise that such a drastic view translated into drastic treatment. Blake advised that all timber had to be removed for not less than 4 feet (1.2m) beyond the extreme limit of the disease to ensure that only healthy timber remained. This was because he believed that the smallest fragment of fungus would certainly regrow. Walls were to be thoroughly brushed down and treated with the alarmingly poisonous mercury chloride or Calvert's No 5 carbolic soap. Ground floors were to be replaced with dense concrete to halt vapour rise and to stop any strands or spores making their way up from the ground. Timber that was removed had to be burnt far away from other buildings to ensure they did not become infected and all tools had to be soaked in disinfectant to kill any spores.

Blake believed that some form of dry rot would be found in most old houses and he stated: 'There are undoubtedly large numbers of old houses, especially in country districts, which are so dilapidated that they would not justify the rather heavy expenditure that would be entailed before the object in view could be accomplished, for any but sentimental reasons' (Blake 1925, 83).

This was the paranoid approach common to the building industry during the early decades of the 20th century and it seems miraculous that so many old buildings have survived.

An academic and eventually experimental-based approach was initiated by the Department of Scientific and Industrial Research, when it set up the Forest Products Research Laboratory (FPRL) in 1925. Its purpose was to undertake research into the utilisation of timber and other forest products. This organisation did not have a laboratory in its early years and the problem of dry rot was given to Professor Percy Groom at Imperial College London. Groom was professor of the technology of woods and fibres.

The result was Forest Products Research Bulletin No 1, *Dry Rot in Wood*, which was published in 1928 and remained in print through six editions until 1960. The later editions were edited by K St G Cartwright and W P K Findlay, who had been Groom's research assistants, and finally by Findlay alone.

It is important to remember that this document was initially a compilation and not based on Groom's research. He did explain how both wet rots and dry rots were caused by fungi, but many erroneous notions that have had far-reaching consequences originated, or were brought together, in Bulletin No 1. These include the ideas that buildings dry down through a zone of moisture content suitable for dry rot; that wet rot turns into dry rot as it dries; that the fungus produces sufficient moisture from the breakdown of wood to sustain it even when the external source of moisture has been removed; and that the fungus carries water to moisten dry timber.

The last idea is still firmly believed by some people today, even by some academics, because the dry-rot fungus produces strands that carry a watery solution of nutrients, but so do the strands of other fungi found in buildings. Long experience has shown that this ability has little or nothing to do with a dry-rot outbreak.

During the Second World War there was a massive increase in decay problems because maintenance became a low priority, bomb damage resulted in saturated masonry and buildings were shut up for years. The problems were compounded by timber shortage, so that available stocks that could have been used for repairs had to be prioritised for essential purposes under the Timber Control System. (Consumer licensing of softwoods was not abolished until November 1953.) The ensuing timber decay and infestation problems were serious and these, together with wartime developments in pesticide formulation, encouraged the rapid growth of the remedial treatment industry.

In 1946 the Forest Products Research Laboratory published *Decay of Timber and its Prevention*. This was Cartwright and Findlay's most important collaboration and was considered the primary textbook on the subject. They, like Groom and Blake, were primarily concerned with killing the fungus within the wall, because they believed that strands could contain a reservoir of nutrients and therefore be a potential hazard for any replacement timber. Effective sterilisation, however, proved difficult. Blowlamps remained popular for several decades. The flame was applied until the surface was too hot to touch, but the treatment was superficial because the necessary lethal temperatures could not be reached in the centres of even quite thin walls. Oxyacetylene welding torches, at around 2,000°C, were tried, but the method had to be used with considerable caution and reliance continued on a range of surface-applied poisons.

Percy Groom had followed Blake in recommending the removal of all decayed timber with a safety margin to ensure that no dry rot was left, but he did not state a specific measurement. Cartwright and Findlay suggested 18 inches (460mm) as a safety margin in their 1946 book, but only 12 inches (300mm) in their contemporary edition of Bulletin No 1.

Wall treatments received a boost in 1951 when Bayley Butler, professor of botany at University College Dublin, recognised the advantages of the masonry bit for wall irrigation. This process required the drilling of holes at intervals to

Fig 58

An example of wall irrigation by drilling and injecting. This method is dubious because walls are never a uniform structure so the distribution of chemicals will be patchy; the quantity of fluid necessary to flood them uniformly would seriously impede drying. Note that there is no timber in the wall shown for the fungus to feed on anyway. The inset shows dry rot growing in an irrigation hole – it is just another humid cavity for the fungus.

about three quarters of the wall thickness, followed by saturation – by gravity or pressure injection – with a fungicide (Fig 58). Butler established his own remedial firm to exploit the technique and it became the standard method of wall treatment in Ireland and the UK. There were still problems. The method didn't burn buildings down but it did fill the walls full of water, and the walls were rarely, if ever, sufficiently free from cracks and voids that uniform saturation was even the faintest possibility, particularly at the 24-inch (600mm) intervals advocated by the FPRL. John Savory (who joined the FPRL in 1948 and later became head of biodeterioration at its successor organisation, the Princes Risborough Laboratory) summed the situation up in 1971. He believed that effective treatment would require so much water-based chemical that drying would be severely impaired and efflorescence caused by considerable salt mobilisation could be expected. Reducing the quantity of fluid used in order to lessen these problems would, Savory suggested, prompt the observation that the method worked best where it wasn't required (Savory 1980).

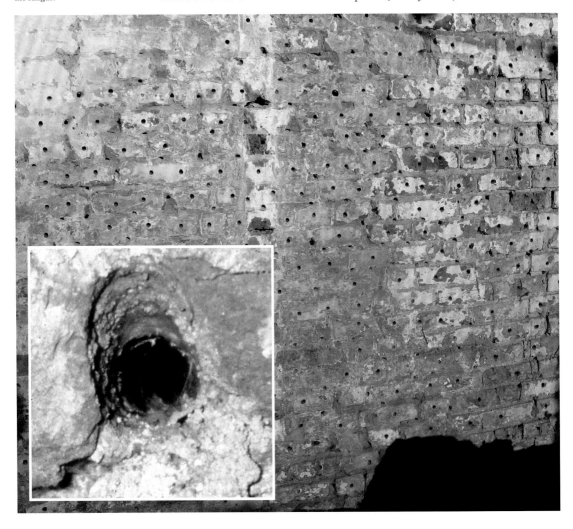

Wall irrigation by drilling and injection should not be used, except under exceptional circumstances. The surface application of a fungicide may be useful because dry rot sometimes produces lots of small fruits as it dies. Fungus strands in the wall, be they dry rot or some form of wet rot, are no problem provided that there is no damp timber available for them to attack.

The chief adversary of post-war dry rot was E H Brooke Boulton. He had been a lecturer on forestry at Cambridge University before becoming technical director of the Timber Development Association (TDA), a post he held for 14 years. In the mid-1940s, he left to tackle the alarming post-war decay problem by establishing a company called Pestcure Ltd (Fig 59). Brooke Boulton carried across the British Isles his message that timber replacement for dry rot had cost the nation £1 million in 1937 and this had risen to £20 million in 1949. *The Bulletin* for 8 June 1949 carried an article entitled 'He sprays death on wood beetles', which contained the following quote: 'The destruction of wood pests in the South is treated as a military operation by several squads of men working under Mr Boulton's direction. Their equipment includes miniature flame-throwers and high-pressure sprays.'

The Chemical Trades Journal for 1 July 1949 reported on a timber 'Brains Trust' organised by the TDA in Exeter in which Boulton gave his justification for drastic dry-rot treatment: 'It [dry rot] drops tears on timber which has a moisture content of probably 14% and then proceeds to weep on this timber until it is over 20% and then goes on to devour it.'

Dry rot is certainly a foe to be feared, but it does not 'weep' unless the surrounding air is saturated, in which case the wood moisture content would be about 28 per cent rather than 14 per cent (*see* Fig 13). This inconvenient fact, however, would not have suited Boulton's agenda.

Fig 59

A Pestcure Ltd stand at an Ideal Homes Exhibition in the 1950s. Pestcure founder Brooke Boulton argued that the harbouring of dry rot should be made an offence unless its presence was notified and treatment was applied – presumably by his company.

The next author to significantly contribute to the debate was Norman Hickin. Hickin was technical director of Rentokil and he wrote several books in the influential Rentokil Library series (including Hickin 1963a and b). His 1963 book *The Dry Rot Problem* stated that all timber should be cut back or removed within 3ft (910mm) of the last signs of fungus (Fig 60), thus ignoring the FPRL and reverting to the ideas of Blake and Brooke Boulton, with whom the early Rentokil was presumably in competition.

We know that Hickin had the FPRL literature, because my copies are from his library, but this was at the beginning of treatment guarantees and he was not going to leave anything that could potentially sustain the fungus. Surprisingly, he did not recommend wall irrigation – perhaps because it had not yet become fashionable. Now that guarantees were being offered, the treatment was always going to cause far more damage than the decay organism. Hickin was a remedial man and his interest was in maximising his company's profits. He was also a dedicated entomologist with a major interest in wood-boring beetles. When I visited him in 1983 he did not seem to have much interest in fungi!

Treatments based on Blake's paranoia and Hickin's marketing instincts continued in a kind of parallel universe to research. Treatment strategies seem largely to have been driven by the requirements of a guarantee, which proved to be a most effective marketing strategy.

Meanwhile, in the real world, Findlay and E C Badcock had shown as early as 1954 that dry rot could not be revived after 12 months in air-dry wood (Findlay and Badcock, 1954). This did not fit well with the idea that dry rot

Fig 60

Comprehensive and expensive dry-rot treatment. The beam has been cut back and the joists, rafters and wall plate have all been replaced. The dry rot that provoked this destruction was historic and dead, but the treatment company insisted on cutting back all timbers to 1m past the last sign of fungus if a guarantee was to be issued.

could sustain itself on water produced by the breakdown of wood alone. This theory had gained support from some work in Leningrad (Miller, 1932), where timber samples had been placed with the fungus in unventilated glass jars. Large quantities of water were ultimately produced by the total breakdown of the wood, but this would be common to all brown-rotting fungi under similar conditions. It was a laboratory-contrived situation that had no relevance to buildings.

Several researchers over the years investigated wood moisture contents and found that dry rot's moisture requirement was no different from other brown-rot fungi. H Viitanen and A-C Ritschkoff, from the Swedish University of Agricultural Sciences, concluded:

> Many experiments have shown that brown rot attack of wood is of no practical significance if the wood moisture content is less than 30%. In this study, however, slight growth and activity of *C. puteana* [cellar rot] and *S. lacrymans* [dry rot] were recorded even at an RH [relative humidity] of 97%, when the moisture levels of unsterile pine and spruce sapwood were on average 25.6% to 26.5%.

Viitanen and Ritschkoff, 1991, 35

If we remember that the wood moisture content in a dry, unheated building will be around 15 per cent, then there must clearly be a significant and sustained moisture problem to support dry rot or any other form of decay.

The final restriction of the term 'dry rot' to *Serpula lacrymans* in 1963 was the work of John Savory. Savory called the fungus the 'true dry rot' but not because of its water requirements – he accepted that these were no different to those of most other brown-rot fungi. The significant difference between wet rots and dry rot was perceived to be that the strands of dry rot (*see* Fig 37) had the ability to grow through walls and over inert surfaces, while the strands of wet rots (those that produced strands) did not. Dry rot could therefore spread through the building where conditions allowed, while wet-rot decay remained localised. Subsequent observations have shown that this is not correct. Most fungi that produce strands have an ability to pass through cracks and loose mortar in walls and over inert surfaces, although dry rot is more liable to do this than most; but fungi that have this ability cannot use it unless conditions are favourable.

This may seem like a technical quibble, but its consequences have been profound. The name 'dry rot' gives the impression that the fungus does not need much water, making it a foe that is going to require drastic treatment. However, its abilities have been severely exaggerated and a comparison between the growth abilities of dry rot and wet rot is presented in Table 1.

Table 1: A comparison between the growth abilities of dry rot and cellar rot (a strand-producing wet rot). Data from Schmidt (2007)

Attribute	Dry rot	Cellar rot	Comments
Strands pass through walls and over inert surfaces	Yes	Yes	Most strand-producing fungi found in buildings have this ability.
Lowest recorded moisture content for feeble growth	21%	18%	Significant decay could not occur until the wood is much wetter.
Minimum moisture content for 2% decay in 8 weeks	26%	21%	Dry rot needs wetter conditions than cellar rot to thrive.
Optimum recorded moisture content range	45–140%	36–210%	Dry rot has been observed growing directly under roof leaks.
Moisture content to germinate a spore and initiate an infestation	>28%	>28%	Free water is required for spores to swell.
Strands conduct moisture to moisten dry timber	Very little ability	Very little ability	Cellar rot may be better than dry rot, but neither fungus can moisten timber more than about 1m from the moisture source.
Walls dry down through a moisture zone that makes them susceptible to dry rot	No	–	If a wall is drying then it is not a suitable environment for any fungus.
Wet rot turns into dry rot as the building dries	–	No	One type of fungus cannot turn into another.

The treatment of dry rot has usually caused far more damage to our building heritage than the fungus itself. There is no doubt that dry rot, growing in a damp and neglected building, can cause considerable decay, but it will still be restricted by the local environment. It will not spread to the dry parts of the house. If I investigate a damp cellar in an old building, I will probably find pieces of old timber that have been damaged by cellar rot or some other wet rot, usually accompanied by weevils and woodlice. This is typical of long-term damp conditions. If I find dry rot in the cellar then it will be because water has dripped through the ceiling or penetrated the walls from faulty rainwater goods or water pipes. There is some other cause rather than just background dampness. It is ironic that a fungus that requires considerable quantities of water to initiate an attack is perceived to be a fungus that requires very little!

A large part of the problem is undoubtedly uncritical observation – we see what we expect to find. If we find dry rot in a dry wall and we believe that dry rot doesn't need much water then it confirms our beliefs and we undertake extensive treatment. If we understand that the fungus needs lots of water then we know that the damage is old and repairs may be all that are necessary.

Wet rots are frequently treated by spraying the surface with a fungicide if the timbers are not sufficiently damaged to require replacement. This is a pointless procedure – at least as far as the fungus is concerned. Decay fungi will be growing within the wood cell walls and a surface application will not halt the attack.

There may be some justification for applying a biocide that will protect the partially damaged timber from subsequent insect attack, particularly if that timber is oak in a building where there is active deathwatch beetle infestation, but a deeper penetration than that obtained by surface spraying will be required.

2.5.2 Rot treatment in the 21st century

By the end of the 20th century, most of the mythology that had driven destructive dry-rot treatment had been disproved. We were now aware of the following:

- Dry rot cannot conduct water to moisten dry timber to any significant extent and its ability is no better than other strand-producing fungus, such as cellar rot.

- Dry rot cannot be sustained by water from the breakdown of timber alone. Its moisture requirements are similar to those of other brown-rot fungi.

- Buildings do not 'dry down' through a moisture zone suitable for dry rot. It needs a significant and sustained source of moisture.

- If dry rot is dry, then it is dead.

However, the requirement for a guarantee still ensured that treatment would be maximised. Wall irrigation retained its popularity and many remedial firms still insist on it to this day. The method began to lose acceptability when the Building Research Establishment published *Dry Rot: Its Recognition and Control (Digest 299)* in 1993, in which it reiterated that wall irrigation should be used only in exceptional circumstances. The treatment of wall surfaces, even with a blowlamp, had some validity but attempting to sterilise the thickness of the wall was a most dubious exercise. Fungus strands are not elastic. The fungus can grow only if it converts a food source into more fungus. Nothing in nature increases body mass without food. A fungus strand within a wall cannot grow when cut off from its food source (damp timber) once the nutrients it contains have been exhausted. Water may keep it alive for a while, but it must die when it runs out of food, even if it is within a few centimetres of damp timber.

The justification for cutting timber back some distance past the last sign of decay had been that the fungus would have spread past the visibly damaged section and be infiltrating the apparently sound wood. However, if the structure was drying and the decayed section had been cut away so that it was isolated from the wall then any fungus left in the wood would die. The Building Research Establishment's *Digest 299* suggests cutting back 250mm, but states that in some cases this may not be necessary. There are, however, still some remedial companies that insist on 1 to 1.5m.

Decayed timber should be cut back to sound wood where this is practical because it will deform as it dries. This is a particular problem with brown rots, which split into cubes because of differential shrinkage. This deformation – perhaps in a door case or interior beam end – will progress rapidly in a dry building once desiccation commences. The decay may have been concealed at the back of the joinery or behind a skin of apparently sound wood and its presence is revealed by deformation, thus leading to the erroneous conclusion that dry rot will grow rapidly in dry timber (*see* section 1.2.3 and Figs 17 and 18).

If deformation does not matter and the damaged timber will be difficult to remove then it can generally be safely retained. Any strengthening required must include an allowance for loss of strength in the apparently sound timber next to the decay. Modern sappy plantation softwoods are generally more easily damaged than original wild-grown softwoods with a high heartwood content (Fig 61).

An approach to treatment assessment that I have used successfully for many years is given in Table 2.

Fig 61
Modern softwood matchboarding has been destroyed by dry rot, while there is far less damage to the original window lining. The two timbers come from the same species of tree but the relatively few years of plantation growing do not allow the tree to develop much mature heartwood and so the modern wood is far more vulnerable to decay. Original softwoods should be conserved wherever possible.

Table 2: A key to the treatment of decay caused by fungi

Start at couplet 1. Choose the most appropriate from 'a' or 'b', then proceed to the next couplet indicated. Continue until a treatment policy is established. Note that all chemical treatments should be used strictly in accordance with the manufacturer's instructions and safety recommendations.

1a	Fungus restricted to the decayed timbers. No signs of strand formation on the timber, on the wall surface or within the wall. No signs of fine red spore dust or dry rot fruits.	Proceed to **2**.
	Fungus producing surface growth and strands that extend onto the wall surface and within the wall, or red spore dust or dry rot fruit.	Proceed to **4**.

2a	Damage minor, or of little consequence.	Proceed to **3**.
2b	Structural integrity of timber impaired or damage severe.	Promote drying. Cut back decayed wood to sound timber and/or consult a structural engineer.

3a	Damage to hardwoods in a building that contains active deathwatch beetle.	Promote drying. Coat damage with a paste preservative.
3b	Damage to hardwoods or softwoods, no deathwatch beetle activity present.	Promote drying. No further action.

4a	Strands appears dead/inactive (grey-brown and brittle) and do not produce condensation when left in a warm place in a polythene bag.	Proceed to **5**.
4b	Strands appear active (white-grey and flexible) and produce condensation when left in a warm place in a polythene bag.	Proceed to **6**.

5a	Building structure is dry. Source of moisture cured in the past. e.g. masonry mc <2%, timber mc <20%	No treatment.
5b	Building structure damp.	Proceed to **6**.

6a	All sources of water located and easily rectified, e.g. faulty downpipe replaced, or little chance that wetting will recur.	Proceed to **7**.
6b	Sources of moisture not obvious or not easily rectifiable. Decay caused by widespread water penetration. Only temporary or emergency elimination of damp source possible – possibility of damp penetration recurring.	Proceed to **8**.

7a	Structure could be left exposed for an appropriate time in order to dry.	No treatment.
7b	Significant time constraints. No time to dry out.	Proceed to **8**.

8a	Cost constraints, or treatment possible only on a temporary or emergency basis; quality of structure or finishes important and/or no opportunity for opening up and reinstating conservatively.	Proceed to **9**.
8b	Structure and finishes apparently less important, or no cost constraints, or structure saturated.	**Treatment A.**

9a	Client prepared to accept small risk of further damage as structure dries. Particularly if timbers are good-quality historical softwood or a hardwood.	**Treatment B.** Monitor.
9b	No risks acceptable, guaranteed treatments required.	**Treatment A.**

Treatment A

1 Remove all sources of water penetration.

2 Remove plaster to expose full extent of fungus. Start from centre of infection and work outwards to edge, but not beyond.

3 Expose any concealed bearings for inspection: on one side if joists, on both sides if thick beams.

4 Cut back decayed timbers to sound wood or coat the exposed bearings with a paste preservative to 0.5m past the last signs of decay. Preservative may need to be caulked into predrilled holes if the timber is thick. If the timber is wet, a preservative formulation based on glycol and boron will give the best penetration.

5 Remove timber lintels within the zone of decay and replace with an inorganic material. (It may be possible to retain hard, old oak if the fungus is a superficial growth, but effective treatment of the oak will not be practical.)

6 Remove bonding timbers, grounds and other embedded timbers within zone of decay. Brick up cavities left by timber removal.

7 Resupport structural timbers as necessary using timber pretreated to BS4072 part 2. The cut ends of pretreated timber should be brush-treated or dip-treated in an end treatment fluid supplied by the treatment company. All new timber should be isolated from the walls with an impervious membrane.

8 Remove window and door joinery within the zone of decay; discard, or strip off paint and repair as appropriate. If repairing, apply two brush coats of a spirit-based preservative to the edges or backs and replace, isolated from the wall as far as is practical.

9 Spray-treat exposed brickwork with a water-based fungicide.

Treatment B

1 Remove all sources of water penetration.

2 Expose cavities as far as practical by lifting floorboards etc and leave exposed for as long as possible.

3 Thoroughly clean out all debris and loose or unimportant decayed material from the zone of decay.

4 Consider the installation of a remote moisture-sensing system to detect any further wetting of the structure.

The following additional measures may be relevant if the structure is softwood:

5 Paste-treat accessible softwood timber to within 100mm of decorated surfaces.

6 Treat embedded timbers by partial exposure and paste application.

3 Wood-destroying insects and chemical damage

All fungi that cause decay in building timbers are part of the natural decay cycle and originated in woodlands. There is no adaptation to life in buildings and if the wood they are feeding on dries and stays dry then they must die. The same approach may be used for wood-destroying insects. These also have their role in the carbon cycle, but their needs and niches are rather more complex.

Regarding chemical damage to wood, it is important to recognise the cause because it will generally be historic (such as smog damage before the Clean Air acts of the 1950s and 1960s) and not require intervention.

3.1 Beetles from the dead parts of living trees

The group of insects that concern us in this habitat are the Anobiidae beetles – the furniture beetle and the deathwatch beetle. The Anobiidae is a widely distributed family of beetles and a handful of species have achieved building pest status around the world. All those that damage wood have similar habits. (They are called powderpost beetles in the USA.)

3.1.1 Furniture beetle or woodworm (*Anobium punctatum*)

The furniture beetle (Fig 62) lays about 30 eggs, each about the size of a pinhead, on rough surfaces, in cracks and crevices, or inside the hole from which the female beetle emerged. These hatch in two to five weeks, depending on temperature, and the young larvae burrow into the wood. Because wood does not contain much nitrogen (necessary for the production of proteins), the larvae grow slowly and it can take three to five years to reach maturity. When they are fully grown (Fig 63), the larvae pupate in a gallery they make beneath the wood surface and emerge from May to early August through a round bore hole as a beetle.

Dead parts of living trees (*see* Fig 9) present an environment that might become quite dry during the summer months and this may have given the beetles an ability to tolerate quite low wood moisture contents. Nevertheless, moisture seems to be important and populations of most anobiid species seem to decline if wood moisture content remains permanently below about 15 per cent. This may be because of a combination of factors. Research has shown that larvae take longer to grow at low moisture contents, that these larvae produce smaller beetles and that smaller beetles lay fewer eggs. A beetle population in a building that is repaired and dried should eventually run out of vigour and die out. This concept is supported by the observation that active beetle infestation is usually found only where timbers are damp. Wood moisture contents that remain below about 12 per cent cannot be tolerated for long, probably because the eggs and small larvae desiccate.

Active infestation is generally thought to be demonstrated by sharp-edged emergence holes and bore dust the colour of fresh-cut timber (Fig 64). These indications need to be treated with caution because bore dust may take many years to darken and the edges of bore holes will take decades, possibly centuries,

Fig 62

The little brown furniture beetle is 2 to 5mm long, with rows of pits along each wing case. The head is tucked under a cowl-shaped cap (pronotum), which covers the thorax. The front of the pronotum rises to a diagnostic peak (*see* arrow), which will be visible using a hand lens.

Fig 63

The larva of the furniture beetle, commonly called the woodworm, is the feeding stage that damages the wood. It is white and hook-shaped, with legs that become non-functional as the insect grows. Damage will be restricted to the sapwood of normal construction timbers.

to become blunt. The presence of the insects is therefore better confirmed by searching for dead beetles (*see* Fig 20) or tightly covering a collection of bore holes with paper or card so that a beetle will punch a hole if it emerges.

Bore dust is generally called frass and is a mixture of fragments of timber chewed by the beetle and pellets of wood that have passed through the insect's digestive system. These pellets may be of a sufficiently distinctive shape to identify the cause of the damage (*see* Fig 64).

Most old roofs have ancient beetle holes, but these are restricted to the sapwood edges because the heartwood cannot normally be attacked. Sapwood damage can usually be identified by its position on the timber, and by the abrupt transition between damaged and undamaged wood. The pattern of beetle emergence holes therefore reflects the way the log was sawn to produce the timber element (*see* Fig 5). If a few rafters show sapwood furniture-beetle damage, it can usually be taken as an indication that the roof as a whole is *not* susceptible to beetle attack.

The significance of this was demonstrated to me by a Victorian softwood church roof in Northern Ireland. The structural engineer had visited the roof and found extensive furniture-beetle damage. Some of this damage, when prodded with a penknife, proved to be about 25mm deep. He therefore subtracted 25mm from each face of each timber component and concluded that the remaining potential thicknesses would not be acceptable – the roof was condemned. Had he understood the damage he was looking at, and the way in which the timber had been converted, then he would have realised that his calculation was not valid and the roof was perfectly adequate. There had been plenty of sapwood edges and the random orientation of the individual components when the roof was constructed gave a false impression of the damage.

Fig 64
When the larva of the furniture beetle is fully grown, it burrows towards the surface and turns into a pupa in a specially hollowed chamber called a puparium. The pupa hatches into a beetle, which emerges via a circular flight hole, 1 to 2mm in diameter, seen in this photograph. The dust produced has distinctive lemon-shaped frass pellets, as seen with a ×10 hand lens (*see* inset).

3.1.1.1 The changing philosophy of furniture-beetle treatment

Ernest G Blake, who we encountered in section 2.5.1, considered furniture beetle to be a small type of deathwatch beetle that was mostly restricted to furniture and decorative woodwork. He did not see it as a problem in construction timbers.

He discusses treatments in his 1925 book and concludes that the best eradication methods are soaking small items of furniture in paraffin and fumigation. The soaked item had to be turned periodically to release air bubbles and this was facilitated by poking a thin wire into the emergence holes. Fumigation was even more interesting. Nowadays we might be a little aggravated by Health and Safety restrictions, but some form of control would probably have been advantageous in Blake's day. Fumigation was to be undertaken in a box with a sealed-down lid, a dustbin with the lid bedded down on putty or in a room with the cracks around windows and door sealed with paper tape. Various fumigants are discussed, with various associated problems.

Blake considered hydrogen cyanide to be the best, but certain precautions were necessary 'to prevent accidents occurring to those who might be in the vicinity'. This presumably included the poor operative who was carefully taping up the door or box lid as the deadly gas billowed forth and the one who had to decide that the gas had dissipated and it was safe to open or re-enter.

Blake viewed carbon disulphide as safer, but noted that it formed an explosive mixture with air. The method of choice seems to have been sulphur dioxide generated from sulphur (brimstone) and instructions are provided.

> The method by which the gas is generated is to stand a pail full of burning coke on a flat stone or a sheet of iron in the centre of the floor and to burn a few handfuls of brimstone in an iron pot or saucepan over the fire. This will speedily give off large volumes of dense, suffocating fumes, and should be left until the room is completely filled, the door being locked and the crevices around the edges pasted over from the outside.

> Blake 1925, 130

This seems a most unpleasant job for the person pasting the edges (though probably less likely than cyanide to be terminal). Blake also recommends that the fire is checked periodically through the window to ensure that burning coals have not fallen onto the floor, though quite what could be done about it if they had remains unclear.

Blake ends his chapter with a warning:

> The futility of dealing with the matter in a half-hearted, haphazard sort of manner should be recognised by the least intelligent person, and if the problem is not given the attention it deserves and is allowed to take its course without any attempt being made to prevent further damage, the blame for future developments would have to be laid on the shoulders of those who were too indolent to exert themselves, when the opportunity for effectively combating the growing danger was presented.

> Blake 1925, 134

Blake did not see any reasons why an attack might be naturally restricted. In his view, if a wood-boring insect was infesting wood, then it would continue until all was destroyed.

Norman Hickin, technical director of Rentokil (*see* section 2.5.1), would have applauded Blake's warning and he became perhaps a little obsessed with furniture beetle. He certainly did not consider it to attack only furniture. Hickin had studied entomology in the evenings while working as a chemist in the rubber industry. In the late 1940s he joined Rentokil, then a very small organisation operating from a shed behind a piano shop in Brixton.

Rentokil was run by Bessie Eades, who had established the company with Professor Harold Maxwell-Lefroy, of Imperial College London, in 1924 to exploit and sell Maxwell-Lefroy's insecticide formulation, which had been developed to combat deathwatch beetle (*see* section 3.1.2.1). Eades continued with the company after Maxwell-Lefroy inadvertently killed himself in 1925 while experimenting with blow-fly control. Her most important contribution was to market the deathwatch beetle insecticide formulation in small quantities for purchase by householders (Fig 65).

Fig 65

An early tin of Rentokil Timber Fluid, retained in his archive by Norman Hickin. These small tins contained Maxwell-Lefroy's insecticide formulation and were sold for use by householders.

Hickin was an enthusiastic businessman, a good entomologist and a prolific writer. He soon became aware that most buildings contained a few furniture-beetle flight holes somewhere within them and he helped to expand the business to include a servicing department that undertook treatments and gave treatment guarantees that were linked to the normal mortgage period. Vigorous advertising included a mobile exhibition and an information centre in Bedford Square, London. The underlying theme was that a housewife did not want to share her home with insects. There were competitors, but Rentokil was probably the leader.

This is a sketch of an industry developing in a different environment to the one that faces us today. It must be remembered that Hickin was responding to a problem exacerbated by decades of construction with sapwood-rich timber, the neglect of two world wars and the commercial availability of powerful new insecticides that people believed could be safely used. These insecticides were effective because they were stable, but their persistence in the environment became their downfall because of fears that they would accumulate until lethal levels were reached in food chains.

Remedial companies flourished and there were soon hundreds of firms throughout the UK which would diagnose and treat timber problems, although with very variable skill and integrity.

Hickin's extensive publications and library demonstrate that he knew all that was known at the time about furniture beetles and this became the knowledge for the industry, but he approached the subject as an entomologist and from a commercial angle. He knew that the beetle laid relatively few eggs and presumably infestations developed slowly. There would not be flight holes until the first generation of beetles emerged from the wood, and these holes would be difficult to find. He also believed that it was many years before timber became susceptible to attack. Absence of beetle flight holes did not, therefore, mean that there wasn't an attack in progress or that the timber would not become susceptible to attack in the future. The answer was a precautionary spray treatment with an insecticide, now called a preservative (another successful marketing initiative). This solution proved to be commercially popular and many people still expect the timber in an old house to have been treated with a 'preservative' when they buy the house, although they only have the vaguest notion why.

Hickin seemed to promote the idea that if a roof was constructed from timber and the timber was of a species that the beetles could infest, then the beetles could destroy the roof. He was certainly aware of the distinction between heartwood and sapwood but he would not have considered selective treatment to be commercially practical or desirable.

A few years ago I was asked to inspect the timbers of a huge 19th-century Gothic building in London. The roofs were constructed from Baltic pine heartwood and the timbers were generally in excellent condition, apart from some fungus damage in the eaves. This was duly reported, with the comment that treatment was not required, but on the next visit people were spray-treating all the timbers. The architect smiled a little apologetically and stated that he thought preservative treatment was a wise precaution. He was a little perplexed when asked what he thought it was a precaution against.

It is generally accepted that spray treatments will not control decay fungi and decay fungi could not damage most of the timbers in a roof anyway because they would not remain persistently wet. The spray treatment of a historic softwood roof is therefore only a precaution against furniture beetle. If the roof contained a large amount of sapwood and there were signs of active beetle infestation then this might be justifiable, but this is very uncommon in domestic roofs that date from prior to the First World War. A few rafters with sapwood damaged by furniture beetle usually means that the roof is not generally susceptible to beetle attack, not that it is vulnerable and requires treatment.

There are situations where surface spray treatments will be appropriate to destroy infestations. These situations might typically be 20th-century roofs or suspended ground floors, where a heavy infestation has become established, or where an infestation has a significant potential to expand and the problem cannot be controlled by environmental modification.

Spray treatment can be expected to work only if the wood surface is exposed. Surface coatings will inhibit fluid uptake and should be removed if not of any historical importance.

Injecting emergence holes with an insecticide at close-spaced (25–50mm) intervals has been popular since the middle of the 20th century (Hickin 1949). This method might be useful for small areas where the finish is important because female beetles tend to return to the hole from which they emerged to deposit their eggs.

The underside of furniture and the insides of draws should always be investigated during an inspection. Fixing blocks used for furniture were frequently of poor quality and animal glues, used for joints and bonding older types of plywood, make a nutritional food source for the beetles. Considerable insect infestations are frequently found in old birch plywood in cellars or attics, and all infested rubbish (stored items that are deteriorating and will probably never be used again) should be destroyed.

Bat roosts, where there are heaps of bat droppings, can also be a good location for furniture beetle damage in floorboards. This is because bat urine is excreted with faeces and this increases the nitrogen content of the wood. (Remember that bats and their roosts are protected by law. Advice should be obtained from a Statutory Nature Conservation Organisation (SNCO) before any works are undertaken that might affect a bat roost.)

3.1.1.2 Furniture-beetle treatment in the 21st century

The acceptance that beetle infestation will mostly be restricted to residual sapwood and that infestations will die out if timbers remain dry can make a considerable difference to furniture-beetle treatment.

Table 3: A key to the treatment of furniture beetle

Choose the most appropriate from 'a' or 'b' and proceed to the next couplet indicated (eg, if 1a is chosen then proceed to couplet 11). Continue until a treatment policy is established. Note that all chemical treatments should be used strictly in accordance with the manufacturer's instructions and safety recommendations.

1a	Beetles present on floors, windowsills, in spider webs etc and/or bore dust trickling from flight holes in timber and/or beetle larvae in decayed wood.	Proceed to **11**.
1b	None of the above present, no unequivocal indications of current insect activity.	Proceed to **2**.

2a	Beetle emergence holes with dark interiors and blunted edges. Damage clearly old.	No treatment required.
2b	All or some emergence holes with light interiors and sharp edges. May be limited recent activity.	Proceed to **3**.

3a	Timber is oak, some other durable hardwood or softwood dating to pre-1900.	Proceed to **4**.
3b	Timber is softwood dating to post-1900.	Proceed to **9**.

4a	Building is dry and well maintained (timber mc <12–14%).	Proceed to **5**.
4b	Building is damp and neglected, or has been difficult to keep dry.	Proceed to **6**.

5a	Components are large and sapwood content low. Damage not significant.	No action required.
5b	Components are small and damage critical.	Repair as necessary.

6a	Building will be repaired, occupied and probably heated. Humidity will usually be below 65%.	Proceed to **7**.
6b	Building to remain empty and unheated for the foreseeable future, or conditions are difficult to improve. Humidity will frequently be above 65%.	Proceed to **8**.

7a	A small possibility of minor further damage while the building dries is acceptable.	No treatment required.
7b	All further damage must be avoided because of decorative finishes or fragile, historically important timber etc.	Proceed to **11**.

| 8a | Sapwood content in timber low. Signs of past or current infestation localised. | Treatment A. |
| 8b | Sapwood content high. Signs of past or current infestation widespread. | Proceed to 9. |

| 9a | Beetle activity can be monitored by tightly fastening tissue paper, or similar, to a representative selection of surfaces where beetle activity is suspected. Leave fastened for at least 12 months. Alternatively, clog holes with wax polish. | Proceed to **10**. |
| 9b | Beetle activity monitoring not possible. | Proceed to **11**. |

| 10a | Holes punched through papers by emerging beetles. | Proceed to **11**. |
| 10b | No holes punched through paper. | No action required until/unless beetle activity confirmed. |

| 11a | Infested items transportable. | Proceed to **12**. |
| 11b | Infested items not transportable. | Proceed to **13**. |

| 12a | Fumigation or freezing facilities available and affordable. | **Treatments B** or **C**. |
| 12b | Fumigation or freezing facilities not available or affordable. | Proceed to **13**. |

| 13a | Finishes can be stripped from the timber, or component less than about 25mm thick with unfinished surfaces accessible. | **Treatment D**. |
| 13b | Finishes cannot be removed, component thick or unfinished surfaces not accessible. | **Treatment E**. |

Treatment A

Brush treatment: Localised areas of infestation without any surface finish, such as paint or varnish, can be flooded with two or three brush coats of any available 'woodworm killer'. Those containing pyrethroids (based on pyrethrum, which is found in a type of chrysanthemum) such as permethrin as their active ingredient are contact insecticides. Others based on boron are supposed to kill the insect if the wood is eaten, but in practice they probably make the wood unavailable to the insects so that they starve. The depth of penetration will be only a few millimetres, although this can be improved with paste formulations.

Treatment B

Fumigation: Facilities using hazardous gases such as sulphuryl fluoride are commercially available to pest control/remedial treatment companies. These, as in Blake's day (*see* section 3.1.1.1), require all gaps around windows and doors to be sealed. Items can be sealed into polythene tents and whole buildings can be shrouded in polythene and treated. Smaller items can be treated in a mobile chamber system using carbon dioxide or nitrogen (which kills by the exclusion of oxygen). These have had favourable reports, and overcome the toxicity problem, but the correct gas concentration will need to be maintained for a longer time.

Treatment C

Freezing and heating: The deep-freezing of furniture and other artefacts in order to destroy infestations is worth consideration. Either a commercial freezer or a temperature/humidity-controlled freezer is normally used, in either case a minimum temperature of −20°C should be achieved.

The items are kept at room temperature prior to treatment so that the woodworm are active. They are then placed in polythene bags containing a little silica gel to absorb excess moisture and positioned in the freezer so that air can circulate around them. A temperature of −20°C or lower should be maintained for 48 hours and it would be usual to monitor with surface temperature probes to ensure that the correct temperature has been reached. The temperature after removal should be allowed to rise slowly over about an eight-hour period while the item remains in the polythene bag. Some authorities suggest that the freeze–thaw cycle should be immediately repeated.

Heating is also a possibility and the idea is to obtain a temperature of 52°C at the core of the timber. This is the temperature at which insect proteins coagulate. The method will be discussed in greater detail in section 3.1.2.2. Static and moveable treatment units are available for small items and immovable items can be treated in some situations.

Treatment D

Spray treatment: All accessible surfaces can be sprayed with a spirit-based preservative containing a contact insecticide such as permethrin or cypermethrin.

Treatment E

Injection treatment: A spirit-based preservative is carefully injected into flight holes at 25mm intervals using either a hypodermic syringe or a can fitted with a suitably constructed nozzle.

3.1.2 Deathwatch beetle (*Xestobium rufovillosum*)

The deathwatch beetle (Fig 66) is closely related to the furniture beetle and with similar habits. It is usually found attacking oak in the UK although it will sometimes damage old softwood, particularly, for some unknown reason, in the Channel Islands. This insect should be considered under Integrated Pest Management, rather than Control because it is usually very difficult to eradicate with chemical treatments without causing more damage to the building than the beetles could. The reason is that the beetles may be behind panelling, in embedded lintels or in beam bearings, where they will be very difficult to reach.

The beetles emerge via round holes, 2 to 3mm in diameter, and produce bun-shaped frass pellets (Fig 67). The female beetle lays between 40 and 60 eggs within the timber via shakes (splits that open as a timber dries) and emergence holes. These eggs hatch in about three weeks and the larvae grow slowly, perhaps for six to ten years or more. The beetles emerge from April to June (although climate change appears to be extending this period). Deathwatch beetles do not necessarily bite their own emergence holes. They may leave the timber via old holes, cracks or crevices in the wood, and mated female beetles will use these to crawl back into the wood again to lay their eggs.

Maxwell-Lefroy (*see* section 3.1.1.1) was probably the first scientist to publish a scientific paper on the deathwatch beetle. In 1924 he observed that many buildings showed historical beetle damage, but there were no longer any beetles. He suggested that if we could explain why the beetles would die out before all the wood had been consumed then we would probably find a control mechanism.

Fig 66

The deathwatch beetle is closely related to the furniture beetle, but is a larger insect, with a length of 6 to 7.5mm. The wing cases are covered with grey and brown scales instead of the furrows and pits on the furniture beetle

The first answer to Maxwell-Lefroy's question, as with the furniture beetle, is that all of the timber is not equally susceptible to attack. A roof may certainly contain active beetle infestation, but that does not mean that all of the timbers are involved.

Sapwood is easily infested, and if the timber is squared from an entire trunk section (*see* Fig 5), there will be residual sapwood and beetle holes on each side. The beetles will not be able to move from the sapwood into unmodified heartwood, so the damage will not be as significant as it seems unless the timber is of poor quality or of small diameter so that the sapwood percentage is considerable. Sapwood damage can usually be identified by its position on the timber and by the abrupt transition between the damaged and undamaged wood (Fig 68). The beetles will die out once the sapwood has been consumed, unless water penetration and fungus provide an opportunity to move into the heartwood.

Large numbers of holes on the surface of a timber will generally indicate sapwood damage (Fig 69), which may become scuffed or disintegrate over the years, leading to an impression of severe damage (Fig 70).

Fig 67

This photograph shows typical deathwatch beetle damage in old oak. Deathwatch beetle eggs, larvae and pupae are very similar to those of the furniture beetle, but the larval growth period may extend to 10 years or more. The inset shows the typical bun-shaped frass pellets.

Fig 68 (above)
The lower pale section of this
ceiling lath is sapwood and
contains numerous beetle holes.
The upper section is heartwood
and the beetles have not been
able to colonise it because of the
natural biocides it contains.

Fig 69 (right)
Typical sapwood damage in a
ceiling joist. There are numerous
holes on one side of the timber.
This gives the impression that
there must be considerable
damage, but any heartwood
present will be hard and sound.
The inset shows a section through
a similar piece. The pale-coloured
dust might lead to the conclusion
that the infestation is current,
but dust takes many decades to
darken and current infestation
would need to be confirmed by
finding the beetles or pasting
paper over a group of holes.

Fig 70
Damaged sapwood falls away
eventually because of scuffing or
vibration. The resulting cross-
sectional loss may have structural
implications but treatment is not
necessary. The damage will be
historic.

Heartwood damage is possible only if the chemistry of the wood and its density have been modified by fungus, and a small amount of decay fungus will radically alter the chemistry. Decay is likely to occur in plates and bearings behind gutters or under suspended floors or in end rafters against gables, and it is in these areas that the beetles will thrive (Fig 71).

Damage will also sometimes be found in the ends of large beams if there was some form of heart rot that was present in an incipient form when the beam was installed. Decay might have progressed until the fungus died when the timber finally dried. The fungus in both of these decay situations does not have to be alive when the beetles infest. Modified timber remains modified.

The second answer to Maxwell-Lefroy's conundrum as to why a beetle infestation would die out when there is still timber available is moisture content. Like the furniture beetle, a deathwatch beetle population will not thrive at a constant timber moisture content that is below about 15 per cent. It is always risking oversimplification to apply rules to population dynamics in nature, but it does seem that drier conditions extend the larval growth period so that smaller adults are produced that lay fewer eggs. However, deathwatch beetles seem to include an added sexual component as follows.

Neither the deathwatch beetle nor the furniture beetle feed. They are just the reproductive and dispersal phase of the life cycle, and it is the larvae that consume the timber. This means that the female beetle would only have the fuel resources she had accrued as a larva, unless there was some way of adding to them. This is accomplished by the male beetle passing across some of his energy-rich resources as part of the spermatophore package when the beetles mate. The male beetle climbs onto the female beetle's back when they mate, but if he is too small (ie, if drier conditions have produced a smaller beetle) then she will shrug him off.

The consequence of these factors should be that a beetle population will diminish (albeit rather slowly) if a building becomes dry and remains well maintained. Sometimes this might not be entirely possible – perhaps in a church on the banks of a river – but good maintenance will still be the key to controlling beetle numbers.

The beetle population, in an increasingly adverse environment, will tend
to become depleted in numbers and split into small colonies where local
conditions are more favourable. It is at this stage, when population numbers are
diminishing, that natural predation should add weight to the decline. The most
important predator in this situation is probably the spider (Fig 72) and even a
small spider will eat several beetles during the beetle emergence season. Spiders
are opportunistic predators that actively search out prey, and they may be killed
by incautious treatment that will have little effect on the beetles.

Hickin and contemporary authors found no evidence that the beetles could
fly and deduced that infestation must have come into the building with the
timber used in construction or repair. The conclusion was that deathwatch beetle

Fig 72
Pholcus phalangioides is a very
common spider in buildings,
where it produces the loose
tangle of threads that form
annoying cobwebs. *Pholcus* is an
opportunist predator and readily
feeds on deathwatch beetles,
which it immobilises by wrapping
in silk (*see* inset).

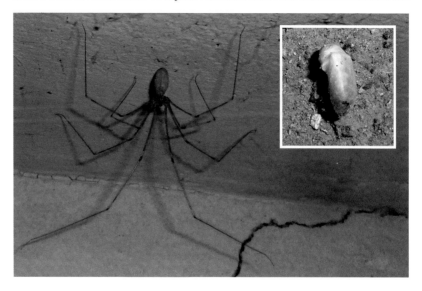

would cease to be a building pest once all infestations had been treated. In fact, deathwatch beetles fly readily if the air temperature exceeds about 18°C; and they provide another interesting example of people not seeing a common event because they are told that it doesn't happen.

Hickin also claimed that infestation was possible via repairs with salvaged timber, but this still requires the building they are introduced into to be a suitable environment for the beetles.

There are plenty of cases of damage in 19th-century buildings that suggest the beetles found their own route in, probably by flying in on warm sunny days. The beetle larvae are common, for example, in the dead branches of willow trees along riverbanks – and migration into buildings may be a problem that will be increased by climate change.

The beetles become sluggish at lower temperatures and many do not seem to move far if they fall to the floor – particularly onto a cold church floor. These beetles may therefore indicate the location and magnitude of an infestation.

Maxwell-Lefroy's conundrum – that there may be timber that the beetles have not consumed but the beetle population has died out – may be explained by limitations on the timber that the beetles can actually attack, and prolonged drying following repair. There are probably other factors not yet identified. Nevertheless, these explanations do show, as Maxwell-Lefroy expected, a route by which deathwatch beetle infestation can be assessed and managed potentially to extinction. If you have a timber-framed cottage or church with deathwatch beetle, then remember that the beetles have probably been there almost as long as the timber. Damage is a slow process and there is time to assess and influence the environment. Good maintenance is ultimately the best method of beetle control, but many other approaches have been tried.

3.1.2.1 The changing philosophy of deathwatch beetle treatment

In 1914 Sir Frank Baines, director of His Majesty's Office of Works, produced a report on the condition of Westminster Hall roof in London. It was found that substantial deathwatch beetle damage had occurred. There had clearly been a history of past repairs, but permanent measures were now thought to be required. Maxwell-Lefroy was asked to investigate and to evolve some method of chemical treatment. His treatment represents probably the first attempt at a scientifically formulated preservative rather than a straightforward poison. The principles, once established, were commercially adopted, but use of the first mixture had to be discontinued because the toxic effects on the workmen were too pronounced (a frequent problem with early preservatives) and a rather safer recipe was substituted. This mixture was applied as a spray in two liberal coats. The second formulation eventually contained cedar-wood oil as a carrier fluid, metallic soap as a poison, dichlorobenzine acted as a fumigant, and paraffin wax held the mix in the timber.

The formulation was elegant and Blake declared in 1925 that the treatment had had 'the desired effect' on the Westminster Hall roof and that 'all life has been destroyed' (Blake 1925, 174).

It was accepted that surface treatments were unlikely to be effective on thick timbers and Maxwell-Lefroy's formulation was considered to be superior because it contained a fumigant, but there is no evidence that it was particularly successful and at least a residual beetle population remained in the Westminster Hall roof. Subsequent wartime bomb damage and unavoidable neglect caused the beetle population to increase rapidly. Yearly totals of collected beetles were kept and in 1960 (for example) 7,345 beetles were picked up from the floor, predominantly in areas that were damped down following wartime bomb damage. Timbers were treated with a variety of sprays and smokes until 1983, but the beetles continued to emerge. The beetle population has now almost been eliminated, but by gutter repairs and maintenance that have dried the timbers rather than by chemical treatments. The interested reader should consult *English Heritage Research Transactions*, volume 4 (Ridout 2001) for a fuller account.

Maxwell-Lefroy's final formulation formed the basis of the first Rentokil fluid, as previously discussed (*see* section 3.1.1.1), and this remained popular until the development of contact insecticides.

The next period of investigation was by Roland Fisher at the Forest Products Research Laboratory during the 1930s. Fisher eventually published four papers that were to form the basis of the industry's approach to beetle control. Unfortunately the deathwatch beetle, with its potentially 10-year (or more) larval period in a piece of oak, was not a cooperative laboratory organism. Fisher's assistant, Ernie Harris, informed me in 1996 that results were put together from scraps of data accumulated over a long time period and that some of the experimental procedure was, of necessity, rather inexact.

The observation that seemed to be most significant was obtained when beetles were put with blocks of wood in glass jars. The beetles laid eggs on the wood, the eggs hatched and the young larvae wandered around for a long time before attempting to burrow. This was seen as a natural advantage to the deathwatch beetle because the eggs could be laid some distance from the most appropriate food source. Spray treatments should be effective because they would kill the beetle when it bit its emergence hole out of the wood; they should kill the eggs when they were laid on the surface and, most importantly, they would kill the wandering larvae. Unfortunately, spray treatments could not be shown to be a success.

Recent research has indicated that doubtful experimental procedure resulted in erroneous conclusions. A high percentage of the emerging beetles make their exit through pre-existing emergence holes, cracks or crevices, so they don't pick up much insecticide and the female beetles re-enter the timber to lay their eggs. Fisher's larvae wandered extensively before burrowing because they were disorientated. They were supposed to emerge deep within the timber.

Surface spray treatments are generally ineffective because the depth of fluid penetration will only be 1 to 2mm. Joinery injectors (one-way valves) are sometimes used to pump insecticides into timbers, but the structure of the wood means there may be good penetration along the grain but rarely across it (Figs 73 and 74).

Insecticide emulsions formulated as pastes probably give a better depth of penetration when spread on the surface or caulked into predrilled holes, and boron/glycol formulations seem to penetrate reasonably well into damp timber.

Boron is an interesting insecticide because it is not a contact poison and can kill the larvae only if it is ingested. It seems more likely that the actual effect is to make the wood unacceptable to the insects and the larvae starve.

Pyrotechnic smoke formulations containing insecticides were shown to be potentially effective but these are not now used and years of trials failed to show that they would eradicate the beetles, although they should deplete the

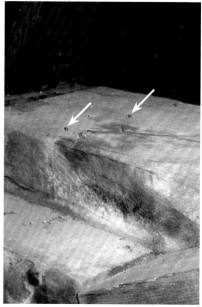

Fig 74

A cathedral in England where two joinery injectors (*see* arrows) were expected to treat a large oak heartwood tie beam that could never have been attacked by the insects.

Fig 73

A church in Belgium where so many joinery injectors have been installed that the roof timbers have been entirely disfigured.

population. Later investigations showed that the beetles could be caught in light traps, but this technique is probably more useful for monitoring and population attrition than for eradication.

Chemical treatment should depend on the severity of the problem and practicalities. Anyone demanding that a beetle infestation is exterminated by a remedial company is likely to be disappointed by both the high financial cost and the extent of damage caused by the treatment. Treatments work best where the infestation is already dead (that is, where they weren't needed in the first place). Treatment failures are generally countered with excuses, and favourite, imaginative ones include:

- The beetles may be alive but they have picked up the chemical as they emerged and will die before they mate.

- The beetles are alive but they have been sterilised.

The problem is that the beetle larvae are usually deep within the wood, and the infested timber is frequently partially or totally inaccessible. A spray-applied chemical will barely penetrate the surface of oak and, despite the protestations of the industry, there is no evidence that it has any impact on a beetle population.

3.1.2.2 Deathwatch-beetle treatment in the 21st century

The first requirement is to ensure that there is current infestation, because the presence of a few beetle holes certainly does not indicate recent activity. Active infestation is usually considered to be demonstrated by accumulations of frass, the colour of fresh-cut timber, trickling from sharp-edged emergence holes (*see* Fig 69). Frass may, however, be easily displaced by building works or other sources of vibration and the surveyor should be cautious. The dust will take many decades to darken and the edges of emergence holes may take a century to become blunt. The best that can be said for these observations, both for deathwatch beetle and furniture beetle, is that there may have been some insect activity during the last 50 years! Frass may also be displaced by small parasitic wasps (Fig 75) and other tiny creatures living in the emergence holes.

A better indication will be to find beetles, either dead or alive, depending on the season. If deathwatch beetle infestation is suspected then carefully search the building. The edges of carpets against walls, the tops of cupboards and windowsills are all particularly interesting if the building is regularly cleaned. Record the positions of any beetles found because these will provide information about the infestation.

Beetles from the previous or current emergence season tend to be intact or alive. Older beetles may disintegrate or be fragmented by other building pests such as museum beetle (*Anthrenus* spp.). This is not infallible, however, and conclusions should be checked by thoroughly cleaning the infested areas prior

Fig 75

Apparent current deathwatch beetle infestation caused by the displacement of frass by nesting activities of a 4mm parasitic wasp (*Stigmus solskyi*; *see* inset).

to the next emergence season so that surfaces can be re-inspected. Remember that deathwatch-beetle damage is a slow process and a year or two's delay for assessment will make very little difference to damage caused by the beetles. It might, however, make a considerable difference to expensive damage caused by unnecessary remedial works.

If activity is suspected, but not obvious, then paper or card can be tightly fastened over the area so that the beetles must make a hole through the covering as they emerge (Fig 76). Ultimately, good repair and maintenance is going to be the best approach under most circumstances, with perhaps localised treatment if a timber is actually infested and enough is exposed to make treatment sensible.

The only method available that should produce guaranteed eradication is heat treatment. This is a method that has been researched extensively in Western Europe. A large computer-controlled steam generator is used to pump hot air into the building so that the surface temperature of timbers reaches 100ºC and the core temperature reaches 52ºC. This should be lethal to the beetle larvae. It would typically take several days to reach the required

Fig 76
Paper can be attached over groups of emergence holes with water-soluble glue. Any emerging beetles will bite a hole through the paper. Pinned card will also work on a surface that is flat enough to ensure beetles do not emerge around the edges.

temperature in the centre of the timber; this would be maintained for a few days and then slowly reduced. Damage to the timber is supposed to be minimised by maintaining the relative humidity at 50 per cent throughout the process.

One company that provides the service mentioned (at an international conference) that they had seen cracks open in panelling – although these closed again at the end of the treatment – and that there were sometimes difficulties in ensuring uniform heat distribution to avoid hot and cold spots. Nevertheless, research colleagues in Germany have demonstrated at the Detmold Open-Air Museum (where there were severe deathwatch-beetle infestations in several buildings) that the technique is effective (Fig 77).

The method is very expensive and attempts to simplify the treatment in the UK have generally produced disappointing results; but this and whole-building fumigation are the only methods that may rapidly eradicate a severe deathwatch-beetle infestation. Neither gives the timber any residual protection, so if some beetles survive and the building remains suitable for infestation then the beetle population may build up again.

Fig 77

Heat treatment to eradicate deathwatch beetle at the Detmold Open-Air Museum in Germany. Timbers are heated to a temperature lethal to the insects, but at a constant humidity of 50 per cent to reduce damage to the timber. The treatment takes several days and is very expensive.

Table 4: A key to the treatment of deathwatch beetle

Choose the most appropriate from 'a' or 'b' and proceed to the next couplet indicated (eg, if 1a is chosen then proceed to couplet 7). Continue until a treatment policy is established. Note that all chemical treatments should be used strictly in accordance with the manufacturer's instructions and safety recommendations.

1a	Holes have sharp edges, light interiors and bore dust (frass) trickling from them. (Beetles frequently present in accumulated bore dust.)	Proceed to **7**.
1b	Holes have rounded (blunt) edges and dark interiors. Any bore dust present may be due to dislodgement through floor or building vibration (eg recent building works).	Proceed to **2**.

2a	Deathwatch beetles or fragments of beetles are plentiful, even though holes look old. (Check windowsills, floors and surfaces below and between building timber. If floors are regularly swept then check crevices and ledges or ask for sweepings to be retained during beetle emergence season.)	Proceed to **7**.
2b	Beetles absent or a few beetles or beetle fragments found.	Proceed to **3**.

3a	No beetles, fragments of beetles, or frass located after a careful search.	Proceed to **4**.
3b	A few beetles or beetle fragments found.	Proceed to **5**.

4a	Active decay still suspected in some localised timbers.	**Treatment A**.
4b	No activity suspected.	No treatment necessary.

5a	Building works have been undertaken during the last decade to halt water penetration or condensation. Structure drying.	**Treatment B**.
5b	No building works undertaken during last decade or water penetration/condensation may still be occurring.	Proceed to **6**.

6a	Beetle or beetle fragments appear randomly scattered. No obvious focus of infestation.	**Treatment C**.
6b	Distribution of beetles or beetle fragments allows them to be associated with individual timbers.	Proceed to **8**.

7a	Current activity widespread in the sapwood edges of timbers.	**Treatment D.**
7b	Current activity in small localised areas or timber bearings and plates associated with walls.	Proceed to **8.**

8a	Timbers are adjacent to or in contact with important plaster so that staining could result.	**Treatment E.**
8b	Timbers are remote from decorative finishes and maximum penetration is required.	**Treatment F.**

Treatment A

Securely and closely fasten tissue paper or similar to small areas where activity is expected and leave over the months of March to July. If beetle emergence holes appear through the papers or beetles are trapped behind the papers then return to couplet 7 in Table 4.

Treatment B

Monitor beetle emergence annually. Ensure good ongoing maintenance. If beetle numbers increase significantly, return to couplet 6 in Table 4.

Treatment C

Seek out and rectify any sources of water penetration. Increase ventilation if practical and acceptable. Monitor beetle numbers annually and try to identify the origins of infestation from beetle distribution and sources of damp. If beetle numbers increase significantly, return to couplet 7 in Table 4.

Treatment D

Ensure that all possible sources of water penetration have been halted. Spray- or brush-treat the infested surfaces with a spirit-based insecticide.

Treatment E

Cautiously coat the top or accessible surfaces of the timbers with preservative paste. Ensure there is no spillage or run-off. The minimum safe distance between the pasted surfaces and plaster will vary in different situations and has therefore not been established. Experience suggests that a good safety margin would probably be about 225mm.

Treatment F

Coat the accessible surfaces of the timbers with a thin and mobile paste preservative. Aid penetration where practical and acceptable by drilling holes at about 100mm intervals to about three-quarters of the depth of the timber.

3.2 Sapwood feeders in freshly sawn timber

Dead parts of trees fall to the forest floor but so, sometimes, do live trees and branches. The nutritious sapwood of a growing tree generally contains too much water and too little air for most insects to attack, but the situation changes as the fallen tree dies and the sapwood dries. This habitat is of interest to us because it is replicated by a wood yard. The insects concerned will be restricted to sapwood because the heartwood (unless of a non-durable species) will not have been modified by fungus.

The digestion of cellulose, a major constituent of wood, is a difficult process, and some wood-infesting insects content themselves with the cell contents, particularly starch. Starch is a storage product which is used up by the time the sapwood (the outer layer of the woody trunk that contains living material) becomes heartwood. Cell-content feeders are therefore restricted to the sapwood of building timbers. Starch also breaks down slowly when the timber has been converted, and these wood-destroying insects are therefore further restricted to timber that is not more than a few decades old.

3.2.1 House longhorn beetle (*Hylotrupes bajulus*)

The house longhorn (Fig 78) or old house borer as it is known in the USA, attacks the sapwood of softwoods, and is a pest in many parts of the world. It probably originated in Africa and was introduced into the UK at the end of the 18th century. The insect belongs to a group of beetles called the longhorns because the majority have very long antennae. Technically they are called the Cerambycidae. Many different longhorn beetles may emerge from timber that has been recently installed in buildings but very few are able to maintain an infestation in that environment.

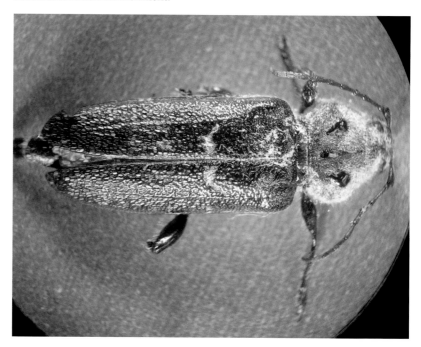

Fig 78

The house longhorn belongs to a large family of predominantly wood-boring beetles called the Cerambycidae. Several species may emerge from construction timbers, but this is the only one found in the UK that can maintain an infestation. The adults vary in length from 15 to 25mm, the female being longer than the male.

The group may be recognised by oval emergence holes (although a few species produce round exit holes), which in the case of the house longhorn are 6 to 10mm in diameter (Fig 79) and usually filled with cylindrical frass pellets. There may be only one or two holes in a rafter but the fully grown larva is rather large (up to 25mm) and substantial damage may have been caused.

About 140 to 200 eggs are laid within cracks on the timber surface. Shrinkage cracks are apparently very suitable. The eggs hatch in 5 to 10 days and the larva burrows into the wood, where it may slowly develop for six years or more. Optimum conditions are said to be a wood moisture content between 26 and 50 per cent, at a temperature of 28 to 30°C.

The fully grown larvae are white with broad, almost rectangular segments behind the head. They can be heard gnawing in the timber during warm weather, when they are most active. When fully grown they pupate and emerge as beetles between July and September. The oval emergence hole is packed with cylindrical frass pellets. An air temperature of at least 25°C is required before they will fly and this is thought to limit the extent of their activities in the UK.

House longhorn beetles are known to frequent buildings in a small area to the southwest of London, but they are sometimes imported in infested timber into other parts of the country and climate change may increase their potential to spread.

The Building Regulations 2010 (Document A, Section 2B) states the following for the areas within the currently accepted distribution of the beetle: 'Softwood timbers for roof construction or fixed in the roof space, including ceiling joists within the void spaces of the roof, should be adequately treated to prevent infestation by the house longhorn beetle *(Hylotrupes bajulus)*' (Building Regulations, Document A, 11). The areas in which this regulation apples are given as:

Fig 79

The larva of the house longhorn, which is about 25mm long when fully grown, takes about six years to develop. The beetle emerges from an oval exit hole that is generally packed with cylindrical frass (*see* inset). The frass has fallen out of the holes in the sample illustrated.

- in the Borough of Bracknell Forest, the parishes of Sandhurst and Crowthorne

- the Borough of Elmbridge

- in the District of Hart, the parishes of Hawley and Yately

- the District of Runnymede

- the Borough of Spelthorne

- the Borough of Surrey Heath

- in the Borough of Rushmoor, the area of the former district of Farnborough

- the Borough of Woking.

House longhorn are generally considered to be a pest of modern timber in the UK and certainly the damage found in timbers dating from the 19th century (particularly in London) is invariably a relic from historical infestation. It would seem that the beetle was then more plentiful. It was first recorded in the UK in 1795, but is now so rarely found outside of buildings that the original wild population is considered to be extinct.

Many other longhorn beetles may emerge from new timbers in buildings, but cannot re-infest. These are collectively referred to as 'forest longhorn beetles'. If an infested timber has dried but the larva it contains is sufficiently large, then it might slowly complete its growth, finally emerging perhaps 20 years later.

3.2.2 Powderpost beetle (*Lyctus* species)

Powderpost (Fig 80) are long, slim beetles (2.6 to 6mm in length) that lack the cowl-shaped projection of the thorax protecting the heads of the furniture beetle and deathwatch beetle. The larvae cannot digest cellulose and they live on starch grains within the wood cells. Unfortunately the pursuit of starch means that the wood cells are pulverised by the large chisel-like mandibles until only sapwood dust remains. The dust does not pass through the insect's digestive system and is not compressed into frass pellets. The resulting increase in volume caused by fragmenting the wood causes its surface to rupture, thus giving the common name of the beetle. The damage is often mistaken for furniture-beetle infestation because both families of insects produce small, round emergence holes, but it is quite distinctive, especially when the absence of pellets is demonstrated with a hand lens (Fig 81).

Furniture-beetle frass pellets feel gritty when rubbed between the fingers, while powderpost beetle frass feels silky. Both insects produce emergence holes that are 1 to 2mm in diameter.

Lyctus species have a worldwide distribution. The only indigenous British species appears to be *Lyctus linearis* Goeze, but a further four species of *Lyctus* and one species of *Trogoxylon* have been introduced.

At least two of the species came from the USA in the years following the First World War. This occurred because large quantities of timber had accumulated, and became infested in American stockyards due to the disruption of shipping during the war. A survey undertaken by the Forest Products Research Laboratory in docks and timber merchants' yards during 1929 and 1930 showed that infested timber was regularly imported from Europe, the USA and Japan. Spread of *Lyctus* was thus attributed to the increase in overseas

Fig 80
Powderpost beetles are about
6mm in length. There are several
very similar-looking species
that live in the fresh sapwood of
hardwoods.

Fig 81
Powderpost beetles produce
round emergence holes in
hardwoods that may easily be
mistaken for furniture-beetle
damage. However, the beetles
start to emerge within a few
months of construction (furniture
beetle infestation takes many
years to build up) and the frass
does not contain pellets (compare
with Fig 64). The damage is
restricted to the paler sapwood.

trade, and threatened at one time to seriously affect the hardwood trade with the USA. The problem was eventually diminished by site hygiene, kiln sterilisation and the use of preservatives.

During the 1940s, *Lyctus* became a problem again and was considered to be the most important wood-damaging beetle in the UK. This, as with the earlier problem, appears to have been because reserves of hardwood were poorly stored for extended periods during the Second World War, and became infested. The restrictions of the war and post-war years then promoted the production of 'utility furniture', which was constructed from every scrap of hardwood available in the wood yard and from air-seasoned logs. Beetle damage became extensive. The preventative spraying of susceptible timber with the new contact insecticides, DDT and later lindane, controlled *Lyctus* in the home and in the wood yard. By the 1960s the importance of the beetles declined, only to emerge again in the 1970s, particularly in hardwood flooring (which frequently incorporated sapwood on the underside so that a hardwood face could be presented as the wearing surface) and in furniture components stored on pallets. Pallets were traditionally made from elm and were frequently found to introduce infestation. The wide variety of tropical hardwoods imported during the last few decades has increased the potential hosts for *Lyctus*.

Hickin (1960) stated that eggs are not laid if the starch content of the timber is less than 3 per cent. If the timber is air dried then much of the starch will be used up in respiration by the ray cells, which remain alive for some time after felling (rays conduct sap across the sapwood). Kiln drying was advocated by the Forest Products Research Laboratory (1962) during the post-war years, and this will destroy any larvae present in the wood, but it also kills the ray cells, so that the starch is 'fixed' within the sapwood. The timber may thus be susceptible to further attack for many years, and any risk of cross infection from other timber must be avoided in the wood yard. Hickin (1945) perceived this problem and recommended that all converted timber and furniture should be treated with an insecticide.

Eggs are laid by means of an ovipositor, which is almost as long as the body of the insect. These eggs are placed by the female to a depth of about 5 to 7.5mm in the early-wood conducting vessels of a large variety of hardwoods, often by biting grooves in the surface of the timber. Only timber species with large vessels can be utilised because, although egg diameter can be varied, the ovipositor must fit into the vessel. This ovipositing behaviour precludes the infestation of softwoods and many hardwood species.

The 30 to 50 eggs hatch within about 8 to 20 days, depending on temperature, and the young larvae at first feed on the remaining egg contents before moving down the vessels. The range of moisture content required is said to be between 6 per cent and 32 per cent depending on species. Under favourable conditions, the adult stage is reached within 8 to 12 months. Adults fly readily and are attracted to light, but infestations usually commence in the stockyard.

Infestations will die out within a few years as the starch within the cells becomes depleted, but historical damage can cause confusion, leading to unnecessary treatment (Fig 82). Solvent or microemulsion-based insecticides and pastes may be useful if there is a large, active infestation.

Fig 82
Typical powderpost beetle damage in the sapwood of a medieval oak rafter. The damage would have occurred within a few years of construction. It is easily confused with furniture-beetle damage but the dust will feel silky rather than gritty because of the absence of frass pellets.

3.2.3 Siricid woodwasps

The siricid woodwasps belong to a large group of plant-feeding wasps that are rather confusingly called sawflies. The female (Fig 83) lays her eggs through the bark using her long ovipositor. This structure looks rather like a sting, but

Fig 83
The giant horntail (*Urocerus gigas*) may have a wingspan of 40 to 50mm. Eggs are laid through the bark of softwood trees with the female's long ovipositor. The larvae grow slowly in the sapwood of softwoods. Some closely related wasps attack only hardwoods.

the insect is completely harmless. The larvae feed on the wood for a period
of perhaps three to six years, after which they pupate and emerge through a
round exit hole (Fig 84). The prolonged growth period means that these insects
sometimes emerge in buildings, where their large size can be alarming. They
are not able to re-infest building timbers.

3.3 Feeders on decaying timber

3.3.1 Wood-boring weevils

The weevils form the largest family in the animal kingdom, with about
60,000 described species. Many are serious pests of crops, stored food
products and forestry, but in Britain only four species occur in building
timbers. *Euophryum confine* and *Euophryum rufum* (Fig 85), both
introduced from New Zealand and first recorded in the UK in 1934 and
1937 respectively, appear to be more successful than *Pentarthrum huttoni*,
the native British species. *Pseudophloephagus aeneopiceus*, the fourth
species, is rather uncommon.

Fig 85

The weevil *Euophryum rufum*.
Four species of weevil will attack
building timbers in the UK, if
these timbers have first been
modified by fungus. The average
length is around 3mm.

Weevils attack hardwoods, softwoods and plywoods, but only in damp conditions where the timber has been modified by fungal decay. Completely sound timber is never attacked and so weevils are classified as a secondary pest. The spread of weevils into slightly decayed timber has been reported, and they have therefore been considered as vectors for the spread of fungus. Water and fungal-decay requirements vary between species. Baker (1970) stated that *E. confine* can live in structural timbers containing only about 20 per cent wood moisture and less than 5 per cent weight loss from fungal decay. *P. aeneopiceus* requires far damper and more intensely decayed conditions.

Studies of the life cycle of *P. huttoni* at 25°C and 95 to 100 per cent relative humidity have demonstrated that the eggs, which are laid in cracks in the timber or holes made by the female, hatch after 16 days. The pupal stage occurs 6 to 8 months later and lasts about 16 days. The adults are easily distinguished from other wood-boring beetles, being almost cylindrical and having the head prolonged in front of the eyes, forming a well-defined snout. They are 3 to 5mm long and brownish-black in colour. Adults live for about 16 months after emergence and can be found all year round. Dead weevils are frequently found in large quantities on windowsills or around lights, and these assemblages suggest the presence of concealed wet-rot decay.

The characteristic damage of all species is recognised by small 1mm-diameter emergence holes and ragged tunnelling along the direction of the grain (Fig 86). Tunnels frequently break the surface of the wood. These

Fig 86

Weevils produce small emergence holes, which may be roughly circular with ragged edges, together with distinctive channelling along the grain. The bore dust contains small frass pellets.

tunnels, created by both the larvae and the adult beetle, are loosely filled with granular bore dust, which is finer than that of *Anobium*. Recent research has indicated that the larvae feed on cellulose and hemicellulose, leaving the lignin to be excreted in the frass.

The larvae are easily killed by drying the infected wood. Adults have a tendency to migrate to other areas when conditions become unfavourable, but this should not present a problem as colonisation of sound, dry wood is not possible. Insecticidal treatment is not required to control weevil infestations provided that the associated fungal decay is arrested.

3.3.2 Crabronid woodwasps

There are several small, solitary wasps in this group that make nest chambers in decayed timber (Fig 87). The nests are provisioned with paralysed insects on which a wasp egg is laid. The larvae feed on the living but helpless insects. The damage can be recognised by pieces of insect among the chewed wood fragments (Fig 88).

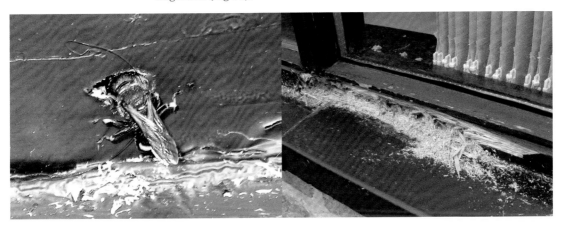

Fig 87

A crabronid woodwasp (*Ectemnius continuus*) nesting in a windowsill that has been severely decayed by a white-rot fungus.

Fig 88

The insect fragments shown in this example are from flies, suggesting that this wasp was also a species of *Ectemnius*. Wood fragments would be coarse and irregular without pellets because they have not passed through the insect's digestive system.

3.4 Bark beetles

3.4.1 Ambrosia beetles (pinhole borers)

Ambrosia beetles belong to the weevil sub-families Scolytinae and Platypodinae. They are generally capsule shaped with various patterns of ornamentation at their head end (pronotum). An example is *Xyleborus dryographus* (Fig 89), which was causing concern in a newly completed house in Sussex, where exit holes were misidentified as a furniture-beetle infestation in recent oak timbers.

Ambrosia beetles are fairly common forest insects in Western Europe, where they attack dead and dying oak trees. Infestations may also commence when a tree has been freshly felled. Infestation will have commenced in the wood yard. It will cease when the timber has been incorporated into a building and the beetles have emerged.

Unlike most other wood-boring insects, it is the beetles rather than the larvae that make the holes and galleries. The female carries fungus spores with her and these grow in the galleries lining the walls. The larvae feed on the fungus (not the wood) and emerge from the tunnel that the parent beetles made. The insects do not eat wood and so there is no bore dust in the galleries. The fragments cut during excavation are ejected from the hole while the beetles bore quite deeply into the sapwood and sometimes the heartwood. Some of the tunnels may be left when the timber is converted.

Ambrosia beetles' exit holes are 0.5 to 3mm in diameter, depending on the species of beetle. These insects cannot attack dry timber and the only holes would be those made by the parent beetle when the galleries were made. The holes may not be particularly noticeable but the fungus lining them will produce dark spores as the timber dries (Fig 90). This meant, in the case of the Sussex building mentioned earlier, that pre-existing holes became

Fig 89

Xyleborus dryographus is a typical example of an ambrosia beetle. The insect is rather capsule shaped, with numerous small punctures at the head end. The length is about 2mm.

Fig 90

Holes and galleries produced by ambrosia beetles may become prominent because the fungus lining produces dark spores as the timber dries. The beetles will have died with the fungus. The beetle larvae feed on the fungus and not on the wood.

highlighted with black interiors, giving the illusion of a rapidly progressing infestation. Sometimes the black-lined holes are accompanied by flame-shaped streaks of discoloured wood.

3.4.1.1 Scolytid beetles
Many of the Scolytinae (Fig 91) feed on the inner bark of trees and do not burrow far into the wood. These leave patterns of surface channelling (Fig 92), which can be mistaken for a current infestation. The insects are of considerable importance to foresters but of no significance in buildings, although the ash bark borer can cause concern.

Fig 91

The ash bark borer (*Hylesinus fraxini*) is a scolytid beetle that lives under the bark of ash trees. It can emerge in large numbers from logs brought into the building as firewood. The tessellated scales on the wing cases resemble those of the deathwatch beetle, but the shape of the insect is different.

Fig 92

Bark borer damage on a rafter. The beetle was feeding on the inner bark and the damage is superficial. Treatment is not required.

3.5 Chemical damage

The surfaces of softwood roof timbers in historic buildings are sometimes found to be a fuzzy mass of sharp-pointed fibres (Fig 93). This is acid damage caused by atmospheric pollution before the Clean Air acts of 1956 and 1968. Damage is particularly common in industrial cities and in buildings where coke stoves were used for heating. The effect is generally less noticeable on oak, which may just have developed a golden colour.

The acid breaks the bonds between the sugar molecules, primarily in the hemicellulose sheaths around the cellulose fibres. Once the sheaths have been degraded, the cellulose fibres are broken into short lengths. The extent to which damage will have occurred depends on the concentration of the acid, the duration of exposure and temperature.

Chemical damage from historical pollution is usually stable and does not require any form of preservative treatment. Localised repairs may be needed if damage is severe.

Most timbers are acidic and some have sufficient free acid (predominantly acetic acid) to attack metal fastenings. This is particularly significant in some more strongly acid timbers such as fresh oak, Douglas fir and western red cedar, which may also cause corrosion on the underside of lead. The problem diminishes as the wood ages, but may return if it becomes damp.

Alkaline damage is rarer but more severe because, unlike acids, the alkali attacks the lignin, resulting in loss of strength and softening. This process has little practical relevance in the normal building environment but is central to the wood-pulp industry for the manufacture of paper.

Fig 93

Superficial acid damage caused by atmospheric pollution before the 1956 and 1968 Clean Air acts. Most of this would probably date to industrial activity during the 19th century.

Glossary

annual ring/growth ring (of a tree)
A year's growth of pale early wood followed by darker latewood produces an annual ring in a pine tree trunk

biocides
Insecticides and fungicides

denature (as in, 'to denature wood')
To change the chemistry and density of wood (eg a fungus can denature building timbers)

differential shrinkage
Tangential shrinkage (tangentially across the width of a tree's annual rings) is generally about twice that of radial shrinkage (which cuts centrally across the annual rings so they appear as a series of parallel lines); this causes differential shrinkage

frass trails
Faecal pellets and wood dust left by wood-boring insects

moisture content
Moisture contents are a percentage of the dry weight; a wet, porous timber can have a moisture content of several hundred per cent

mycologist
A scientist who studies fungi

phenolic chemicals
Chemicals based on phenols (a hydroxyl group bonded to an aromatic hydrocarbon group)

phenolic molecules
Phenolic molecules make phenolic chemicals

relative humidity
The amount of water the air is holding at a particular temperature as a percentage of the water it would contain at that temperature if saturated

Bibliography

Baker, J M 1970 'Wood-boring weevils in buildings'. *Timberlab News* **4**, 6–7

Blake, E G 1925 *Enemies of Timber, Dry Rot and Deathwatch Beetle*. London: Chapman & Hall

Building Research Establishment 1972 *Laboratory Tests on Natural Decay Resistance in Timber*. Timberlab Paper 50. Princes Risborough: Forest Products Research Laboratory

Building Research Establishment 1993 *Dry Rot: Its Recognition and Control*, Digest 299. Watford: Building Research Establishment

Cartwright, K St G and Findlay, W P K 1946 *Decay of Timber and its Prevention*. London: HMSO

English Heritage 2012 *Practical Building Conservation – Timber* (eds McCaig, I and Ridout, B V). London: Ashgate

Findlay, W P K 1953 *Dry Rot and Other Timber Troubles*. London: Hutchinson's Scientific and Technical Publications

Findlay, W P K and Badcock, E C 1954 'Survival of dry rot in air-dry wood'. *Timber Technology* **62**, 137–38

Forest Products Research 1928 *Dry Rot in Wood*, Bulletin No 1. London: HMSO

Forest Products Research Laboratory 1962 *The Kiln Sterilization of Lyctus Infested Timber*, Leaflet 13. Princes Risborough: Forest Products Research Laboratory

Hickin, N E 1945 '*Lyctus*: The enemy of home grown oak'. *The Cabinet Maker and Complete House Furnisher*, 25 August, 193–94

Hickin, N E 1949 'Woodworm in structural timbers'. *The Illustrated Carpenter and Builder*, 10 June

Hickin, N E 1960 'An introduction to the study of the British Lyctidae'. *Record of the 1960 Annual Convention of the British Wood Preserving Association*, 57–83

Hickin, N E 1963a *The Dry Rot Problem*. London: Hutchinson & Co

Hickin, N E 1963b *The Insect Factor in Wood Decay*. London: The Rentokil Library, Associated Business Programmes (3 edn, 1975)

Johnson, J 1795 *Some Observations on that Distemper in Timber Called Dry Rot*. London

Maxwell-Lefroy, H 1924 'The treatment of the deathwatch beetle in timber roofs'. *Journal of the Royal Society of Arts* **52**, 260–66

Miller, U V 1932 *Points in the Biology and Diagnosis of House Fungi*. State Leningrad: Forestal Technical Publishing Office

Ridout, B V 2000 *Timber Decay in Buildings: The Conservation Approach to Treatment*. London: E & F N Spon

Ridout, B V 2001 'The population dynamics of the deathwatch beetle, and how their mode of attack influences surface treatments, as demonstrated by Westminster Hall, London'. *English Heritage Research Transactions* **4**, 2–39

Savory, J G 1971 *Dry Rot – Causes and Remedies*. Timberlab Paper 44. Princes Risborough: Forest Products Research Laboratory

Savory, J G 1980 'Treatment of outbreaks of dry rot (*Serpula lacrymans*)'. *British Wood Preserving Association News Sheet 160* (May)

Schmidt, O 2007 'Indoor wood – decay basidiomycetes: damage, causal fungi, physiology, identification and characterization, prevention and control'. *Mycological Progress* **6**, 261–79

Viitanen, H and Ritschkoff, A-C 1991 *Brown Rot Decay in Wooden Constructions: Effect of Temperature, Humidity and Moisture*. Swedish University of Agricultural Science, Department of Forest Products, Report No 222

Index